WINNING CHESS OPENINGS

LEARN 25 ESSENTIAL OPENING STRATEGIES TODAY!

T0020605

ABOUT THE AUTHOR

Bill Robertie is the world's best backgammon player and the only two-time winner of the Monte Carlo World Championships. Robertie is the author of seven backgammon books and the co-publisher of *Inside Backgammon*, the leading backgammon magazine. He also is a chess master, winner of the U.S. Speed Chess Championship, and the author of six chess books. Robertie's club and tournament winnings have allowed him to travel the world in style. He currently makes his home in Arlington, Massachusetts.

BACKGAMMON AND CHESS BOOKS BY BILL ROBERTIE

501 Essential Backgammon Problems
Backgammon for Winners
Backgammon for Serious Players
Advanced Backgammon Volume 1: Positional Play
Advanced Backgammon Volume 2: Technical Play
Lee Genud vs. Joe Dwek
Reno 1986
Beginning Chess Play
Winning Chess Tactics
Winning Chess Openings
Master Checkmate Strategy
Basic Endgame Strategy: Kings, Pawns, & Minor Pieces
Basic Endgame Strategy: Queens and Rooks

WINNING CHESS OPENINGS

LEARN 25 ESSENTIAL OPENING STRATEGIES TODAY!

BILL ROBERTIE

CARDOZA PUBLISHING

2022 EDITION

Copyright © 1995, 2002, 2018, 2022 by Bill Robertie
- All Rights Reserved -

ISBN 13: 978-1-58042-394-6

Visit our website or write for a full list of Cardoza Publishing books and advanced strategies.

CARDOZA PUBLISHING
www.cardozapublishing.com

TABLE OF CONTENTS

INDEX OF OPENINGS

INDEX OF PLAYERS

1

INTRODUCTION

In this book, we'll show you the opening secrets of the chess masters and how to apply them in your own games. From the standard King's Pawn, to the counterattacking half-open defenses, we go over the 25 most essential openings in chess.

FIRST WORD

Chess is the world's greatest strategy game, played on every continent and in every country. It's complex, exciting, and fun, and there's no thrill quite like that of outmaneuvering a tough opponent and watching him turn over his King in capitulation!

The openings we show here cover the gamut of play, from the popular and very powerful Ruy Lopez and sizzling Sicilian Defense, to more unusual starters like the King's Indian and the Queen's Gambit-Slav Defense, openings that will stun opponents and keep them on edge.

You'll learn how to play aggressive, dynamic openings as White and Black, the thinking behind each of the openings, and how to control the play so that opponents are kept on the defensive while you push for victory. We go over king's pawn and queen's pawn openings, classic center games, asymetrical defenses, fianchettos, gambits, and much more.

Each opening is fully discussed with the thinking shown from both white's and black's perspectives, and the possibilities of moves and their strengths (and weaknesses) fully played out.

By the time you finish this book and study the wealth of plays, all fully annotated and shown, you'll be ready to seize the advantage over opponents, and be a winner at chess!

.

2

CHESS NOTATION

Chess notation starts by putting a coordinate grid over the chessboard. Take a look at the diagram below. The horizontal rows, or **ranks**, are numbered from 1 to 8. White's first row, the rank containing the White pieces, is number 1. The rank with Black's pieces now number 8. The verti-

FIRST WORD

Chess notation is a simplified way of recording the moves in a chess game. By learning notation, you'll be able to follow games and explanations in all chess books. It's really easy. Here's how it works.

cal rows, or **files**, are lettered **"a"** through **"h"**, with "a" starting on White's left and "h" on White's right.

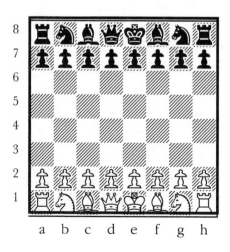

9

This grid system lets us refer to any square on the board. White's King is currently sitting on the square "e1". Black's Queen is on square "d8", and so on.

In addition to the grid system, we have abbreviations for each of the pieces. Here they are:

ABBREVIATIONS FOR THE PIECES	
King	K
Queen	Q
Rook	R
Bishop	B
Knight	N
Pawn	-

To indicate a move, we write down the piece that moved, and the starting and ending squares of the move. However, if a pawn is moving, we don't write anything more than the starting and ending squares. We use a dash to separate the starting and ending squares, and an "x" if the move was a capture.

SPECIAL NOTATIONS

Certain moves in chess have their own special notation.

• Castling King-side is denoted by "0-0". Castling Queen-side is denoted by "0-0-0".

• When promoting a pawn, indicate the promoted piece in parentheses: for instance, "a7-a8 (Q)" says that White moved a pawn to the a8 square and promoted it to a Queen.

• Capturing *en passant* is indicated by "ep" after the move: for instance, "d5xc6 ep" shows a pawn capturing *en passant* on the c6 square.

We use exclamation points and question marks to comment on the ingenuity or effectiveness of moves. Here's what they mean:

ANNOTATION COMMENTS

! means a good move.
!! means a brilliant, completely unexpected move.
? means an error.
?? means a gross blunder, probably losing the game.

3

WINNING IDEAS IN THE CHESS OPENINGS

Although there are many chess openings, many with exotic and odd-sounding names, they're all united by a few common principles. Let's take a look.

In general, we have two strategic goals in mind when playing the opening of a chess game. The first is development - the opening is the time to get our pieces into play. The second is pawn structure - we want a favorable formation of our center pawns, which will be the foundation on which we'll build our middle game attack.

> ### FIRST WORD
> The *opening* in chess refers to the early moves of the game, when the armies are being mobilized for battle. Everything known about opening a chess game is called *opening theory*.
>
> Let's see what that is.

The player who combines good development with a sound pawn structure is the player most likely to triumph in the middle game battle.

DEVELOPMENT

Development is the process of getting your pieces off the first rank and into battle, and contesting the vital center squares. The opening of the game is the time when development takes place, and the winner in the development race, the player who gets his army mobilized first, is the player most likely to win the game.

There are some good general rules that serve as a guide for developing your pieces. Follow these rules, and you can't go too far wrong in the opening. Here they are:

PRINCIPLES OF DEVELOPMENT

• Advance the d- and e-pawns, two squares if possible, to clear the way for the other pieces.

• Develop the Knights before the Bishops, preferable to f3, c3, c6, and f6.

• Develop the Bishops next, to active squares if possible, defensive squares if necessary.

• Castle, to safeguard the King and develop the Rook.

• Move the Queen off the first rank but not too far from home, to avoid being harassed by the opponent's pieces.

• Develop the Rooks to squares on the central files (c1, d1, e1, and f1 for White, and the corresponding squares for Black). These files are likely to be opened later in the game, and the Rooks will then come into play.

• When possible, try to develop with a *threat:* if your opponent can't meet the threat with a developing move of his own, you will gain time in the race to get the pieces out.

These are general rules, and not every rule will apply in every opening. Sometimes a tactical necessity will force you to deviate from this well-ordered list. But for the most part, following these rules will ensure that you emerge from the opening with a playable game.

Let's take a look at the opening of a game where White follows these rules closely while Black ignores them.

1	e2-e4	d7-d6
2	d2-d4	c7-c6
3	Nb1-c3	g7-g6
4	Ng1-f3	Bf8-g7
5	Bf1-c4	Ng8-f6
6	Qd1-e2	0-0
7	0-0	Nb8-a6
8	Bc1-f4	Na6-c7
9	e4-e5	Nf6-e8

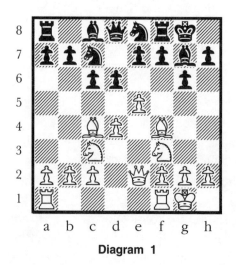

Diagram 1

White hasn't done anything special. He's simply developed his pieces, closely following our rules. Once he brings his Rooks to the center of the board, he'll have completed his development.

Black, on the other hand, has violated almost all our rules - and look at the consequence! His pieces are now confined to the first two rows, tripping over each other. Once the position opens up, will Black be able to withstand White's attack? Possible, but doubtful. Black has lost control of the center, and the prospects now all belong to White.

The secret of successful opening play is to look for ways to advance your own development while hindering your opponent's. As you play through the openings in this book, notice how each side tries to do this.

PAWN STRUCTURE

The second goal of opening play is to achieve a favorable pawn structure - one which will give you an advantage in space in the maneuvering that will follow the opening, or one which will permit you to attack your opponent's weaknesses more easily than he can attack yours.

What do we mean by a favorable pawn structure? Let's start by looking at an *ideal* pawn structure - one which White would like to attain but usually cannot.

The next two diagrams show variations of an ideal pawn structure for White:

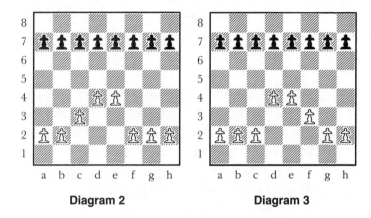

Diagram 2 Diagram 3

A word about these diagrams. We've eliminated the pieces on both sides, because for right now we're concentrating on just the placement of the pawns. And we haven't shown any pawn moves for Black yet. That's because an ideal pawn center for White is one where Black hasn't contested the center. What makes these structures ideal? Two factors:

1. White controls the entire center with his two pawns abreast on e4 and d4. Whoever controls the **center** - squares c4, d4, e4, f4, c5, d5, e5, f5 - dictates the course of the game.

2. White's center has maximum potential - that is, White is free to advance either his e-pawn or his d-pawn, depending on circumstances.

This last point, the potential of the center, is very important. For instance, compare the last two diagrams to the next one:

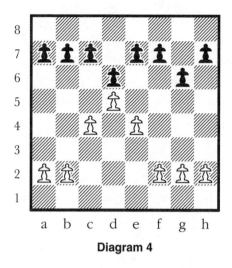

Diagram 4

Now answer this question: Is Diagram 4 better or worse for White than Diagram 2?

Most beginners would answer that Diagram 4 must be better. After all, White has advanced his c-pawn and his d-pawn one additional square each, thereby grabbing more space. Isn't it good to have more space?

The answer, however, is that Diagram 4 is actually worse for White than Diagram 2. Although White has more space, the potential of his center has been greatly reduced. None of his center pawns are able to advance without being captured, while he has lost control of all the dark squares in the center - c5, d4, and e5. Black can now use these squares to post his pieces aggressively.

In Diagram 2, by contrast, Black has no secure squares in the center for his pieces. Paradoxically, although the strength of Diagram 2 lies in White's ability to move his

17

pawns in any way he chooses, once he actually moves the pawns, his formation loses energy and Black is able to occupy the spaces left behind. As a consequence, White wants very much to retain the formations of Diagrams 2 and 3 as long as he can, moving the pawns only when that guarantees him some lasting advantage.

In practice, White is unable to obtain the perfect formations of Diagrams 2 and 3, since Black will want to fight for the center as well. The best formation that White is actually able to achieve in practice is something like Diagram 5:

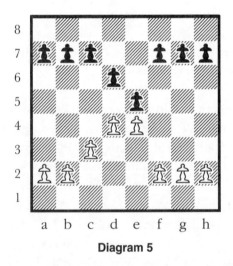

Diagram 5

(Diagram 5 results from a King's pawn opening where White opens with e2-e4 and Black replies with e7-e5. After some maneuvering, White is often able to achieve this pawn structure by playing c2-c3 followed by d2-d4.)

Diagram 5 is quite favorable for White, since his pawns deny Black any good piece placements in the central

18

area, while White benefits from the slight advantage in space. If, as the White player, you can achieve and hold on to a position like Diagram 5, your prospects in the game should be very good.

In most games, however, this pawn structure can't be preserved forever. At some point, a push or an exchange will result. Let's look at the pawn structures that can develop from Diagram 5. Basically, Diagram 5 can change in one of three ways:

    1. White can exchange pawns.
    2. White can advance his d-pawn to d5.
    3. Black can exchange pawns.

Diagram 6 shows the position after White's exchanged pawns.

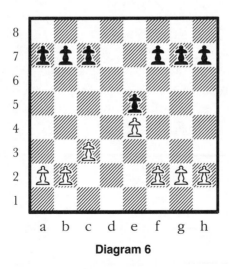

Diagram 6

This pawn position is now equal. Neither side has any advantage, and this is a good result for Black, whose job in the opening is to try to equalize the game. In most cases, the open d-file will eventually lead to an exchange of the Rooks and possibly the Queens. Diagram 7 shows the position after Black challenges the center with c7-c5 and White pushes his d-pawn to d5.

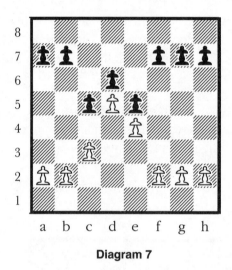

Diagram 7

Slight edge for White, who has more space. He may also be able to maneuver one of his Knights to c4, where it will attack the weak pawn on d6. Black will aim for counterplay with f7-f5 or b7-b5.

Finally, Diagram 8 shows the position after Black exchanges in the center with e5xd4.

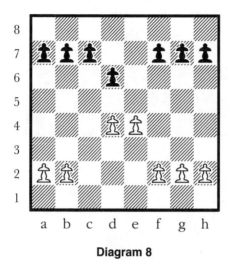

Diagram 8

This is the best result for White, who now has a sizeable advantage. Black's goal here is to weaken the White center by attacking with either c7-c5 or d7-d5.

As you play through the openings described in the rest of the book, keep the key pawn structures in mind. Much of the strategic play in the openings is an attempt to attain a favorable pawn structure for the subsequent middle game.

4

DOUBLE KING-PAWN OPENINGS

Double King-Pawn openings are those in which the players begin by moving their King pawns two squares forward. White plays e2-e4 on his first move, and Black responds with e7-e5, resulting in the position on the following page.

We'll look at all the double King-pawn openings here except the **Ruy Lopez**. That opening is more popular than all the others put together, so we'll look at it separately in the following chapter.

FIRST WORD

If Black doesn't know what he's doing, these openings can give White powerful attacks very quickly. Among grandmasters, it's assumed that Black knows how to handle these openings. But don't make these assumptions about players you'll face! These openings are dangerous weapons.

In the 19th century, the double king's pawn openings were the mainstays of master chess. Nowadays they aren't seen much at the top level of play, although they can be dangerous among amateurs. They aren't popular now because, if Black knows what he's doing, White's first move advantage can be dissipated quickly. The key, however, is *if Black knows what he's doing.*

Diagram 9

In this chapter we'll look at these openings:
- **Center Game**
- **Danish Gambit**
- **Bishop's Opening**
- **Giuoco Piano**
- **Evans Gambit**
- **King's Gambit**
- **Four Knight's Game**

THE CENTER GAME

We said earlier that White's primary strategic goal in the opening was to establish the classical pawn center: two pawns abreast at e4 and d4. In the **Center Game**, White tries to establish this pawn center at the first available opportunity: the second move.

The Center Game is for players looking for open piece play with no sacrifice of material. White will maintain a slight advantage in space, although with correct play, Black will be able to develop his pieces without difficulty.

Diagram 10

	White:	Black:
1	e2-e4	e7-e5
2	d2-d4	...

The Center Game isn't a subtle opening. White knows what he wants and goes for it directly.

2	...	e5xd4

This is the problem with the Center Game. By exchanging pawns immediately, Black forces White to recapture with his Queen, thus violating one of the primary rules of opening play: *Don't bring out your Queen prematurely.*

24

3   Qd1xd4

White has to recapture or be a pawn down.

3   ...   Nb8-c6

Black develops his Knight to an ideal square and chases the White Queen away from its central post. White loses a whole move, which in the opening is usually enough to allow Black to get an equal game.

4   Qd4-e3   ...

Although this move blocks the development of the Queen's Bishop somewhat, the Queen really has no ideal square to go to. Moving to d3 blocks the King's Bishop, and d1 is an abject retreat. Worst of all is Qd4-c3??, which loses the Queen immediately to the pin Bf8-b4!

4   ...   Ng8-f6

Black develops his other Knight, following a good general rule: *Knights before Bishops*.

5   Nb1-c3   ...

Protects the e-pawn, and helps prevent Black's natural freeing move in most King's pawn openings, d7-d5. When Black can play that move with impunity, he gets a free and easy game.

5   ...   Bf8-b4

Develops the Bishop, pins the Knight to the King, and prepares to Castle.

6	Bc1-d2	...

Breaks the pin and prepares to Castle on the Queen-side, White's usual plan in this opening.

6	...	0-0
7	0-0-0	Rf8-e8

Activates the Rook and attacks White's e-pawn. White must be careful, as the pawn is now pinned against the Queen behind it.

8	Bf1-c4	d7-d6
9	Ng1-f3	Bc8-e6!

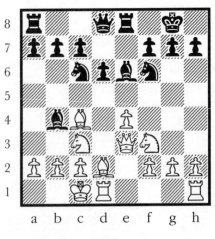

Diagram 11

Black has a comfortable development with no problems. The awkward position of White's Queen in the center makes it difficult for him to work up any initiative. White has a choice between exchanging Bishops on e6, pinning Black's Knight with Bc4-b5, or retreating with Bc4-b3. All lead to about an even game. Black should proceed with his development, bringing his Queen into play on d7 and moving his other Rook to d8.

THE DANISH GAMBIT

The **Danish Gambit** is a swashbuckling attempt to improve on the Center Game by sacrificing a pawn or two. The basic position is this:

	White:	Black:
1	e2-e4	e7-e5
2	d2-d4	e5xd4
3	c2-c3	...

Diagram 12

Instead of recapturing as in the Center Game, White offers a genuine pawn sacrifice, to gain time and clear open lines for his Queen and Bishops. If Black defends carefully, he can equalize or even gain the advantage. If he defends carelessly, he can be overrun quickly.

The Danish Gambit is a fine choice for White players who want wide-open lines with plenty of attacking chances, and who don't mind sacrificing a couple of pawns on the way. White will get plenty of scope for his ideas, but he will have to outplay his opponent to crash through to victory. If Black can weather the storm, his extra pawns will win in the endgame.

3	...	d4xc3

An old chess adage says, *The best way to refute a gambit is to accept it.* Black can also get a good game, with considerably less risk, by playing d7-d5.

4	Bf1-c4	...

White offers a second pawn to accelerate his development.

4	...	c3xb2
5	Bc1xb2	Bf8-b4 check

The Austrian grandmaster Schlechter, who lost a close match for the World Championship in 1910 to Emanuel Lasker, invented the defense d7-d5 at this point, which gives back a pawn to ease Black's development. It's the main reason the Danish Gambit is rarely seen these days.

Checking with the Bishop is an older variation, which will serve to illustrate the Gambit's attacking power against inaccurate defense.

| 6 | Ke1-f1 | ... |

White sacrifices his Castling option to keep as many pieces on the board as possible.

| 6 | ... | Ng8-f6 |

Develops a piece and guards the pawn on g7, which was threatened by the Bishop on b2.

| 7 | e4-e5! | ... |

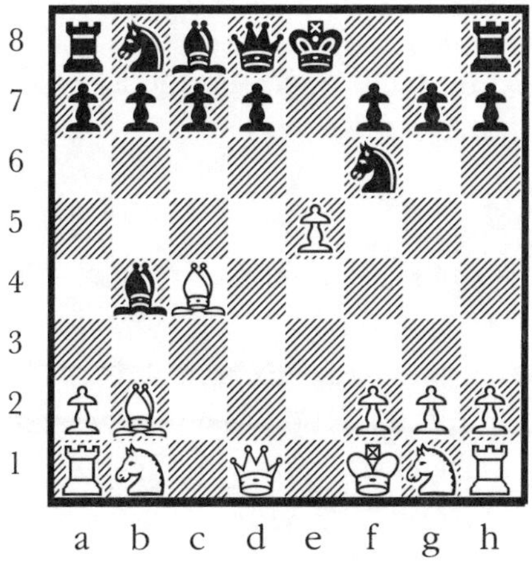

Diagram 13

Attacks the Knight, which has few squares available.

| 7 | ... | d7-d5 |

Black responds by counterattacking the Bishop. If Black moves the Knight to e4 (the only safe square available other than g8), White has the powerful response Qd1-d5! attacking the loose Knight and threatening mate at f7.

8	Bc4-b5 check	Nf6-d7
9	Qd1-g4 ·	...

A new attack on the pawn at g7 and the Bishop on b4. White's threats are starting to mount.

9	...	Bb4-f8

The only way to guard both pieces.

10	e5-e6!	...

Attacks the Knight and opens up the long diagonal for the Bishop on b2.

10	...	f7xe6
11	Qg4-h5 check!	Ke8-e7

Black's other choice is g7-g6, after which White plays Qh5-h3, and the Black Rook at h8 is threatened by the Bishop on b2. If Black defends with Rh8-g8, then Qh3xe6 check wins the Rook.

12	Bb2-a3 check	c7-c5
13	Ba3xc5 check!	Nd7xc5
14	Qh5-g5 check!	

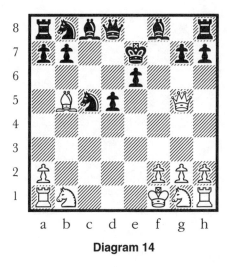

Diagram 14

Whether Black moves the King to f7 or d6, White replies with Qg5xd8, with a winning position. White will have a material advantage of a Queen for a Bishop, and will eventually be able to use his powerful Queen to win still more material.

BISHOP'S OPENING

The **Bishop's Opening** for White is a good choice if you like open lines and easy development without any speculative sacrifices. It is characterized by the development of White's King's Bishop to the c4 square on the second move:

	White:	Black:
1	e2-e4	e7-e5
2	Bf1-c4	

Diagram 15

The Bishop's move accomplishes two purposes beyond simply getting a piece off the back rank: it strikes at the f7 square, Black's weak spot in the King pawn openings, and it prevents Black (for now) from playing d7-d5, which as we've seen so far can be a key freeing move for Black.

White's long-range plan is to play d2-d3, supporting his King-pawn, and then f2-f4, expanding on the King-side. This amounts to playing a King's Gambit without the gambit.

2	...	Ng8-f6

This is the **Berlin Defense**, which caused the Bishop's Opening to more or less vanish from master play. Black gains time by attacking the undefended e-pawn.

3	d2-d3	...

The most solid continuation. Another idea is the daring gambit d2-d4, which leads to great complications.

| 3 | ... | c7-c6! |

Black prepares a later strike in the center with d7-d5.

| 4 | f2-f4 | ... |

White continues with his plan, but it doesn't promise much.

| 4 | ... | e5xf4 |
| 5 | Bc1xf4 | d7-d5 |

The counterattack in the center frees Black's pieces and guarantees him at least an even game.

| 6 | e4xd5 | Nf6xd5 |

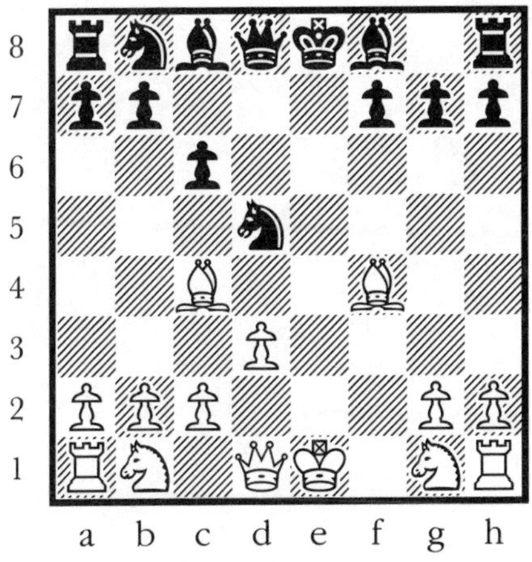

Diagram 16

The Knight gains time by attacking the loose White Bishop, which must now retreat.

White will play moves like Bf4-g3, Ng1-f3, and 0-0 to get his pieces into the game. Black will develop with Bf8-c5 or e7, 0-0, and Bc8-g4 or f5. White will try to mount an attack down the f-file, which Black will be prepared to repel. The chances are about equal.

GIUOCO PIANO

In Italian, *Giuoco* means game and *piano* means quiet, so Giuoco Piano translates as *quiet game*. (In Europe, it's known simply as the *Italian Game*.) The **Giuoco Piano** was the first opening to be analyzed extensively. Italian manuscripts of the sixteenth and seventeenth centuries give analysis by players like Greco and Damiano, the strongest players of their day.

The Giuoco Piano begins like this:

	White:	Black:
1	e2-e4	e7-e5
2	Ng1-f3	Nb8-c6
3	Bf1-c4	Bf8-c5

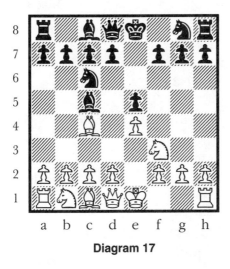

Diagram 17

White's second move, Ng1-f3, attacks Black's e-pawn. This restrains Black's choices somewhat, so he brings out his Knight on b8 to defend the pawn. Both sides then develop their King's Bishop, striking at the weak points on f7 and f2, respectively.

The Giuoco Piano is a good opening to play if you feel your opponent is spoiling for a fight from the first move. The quiet nature of the play postpones the main action until the middle game, and your opponent may not have the patience required. Be warned, however: if Black plays alertly and is happy to simplify, you may have a hard time working up any pressure. Let's follow a typical variation and see how it goes.

4   Nb1-c3   ...

White develops in a straightforward fashion, bringing his pieces out to their best squares in the center.

| 4 | ... | Ng8-f6 |

Black does the same.

| 5 | d2-d3 | ... |

The d-pawn moves so White can develop his Queen's Bishop.

| 5 | ... | d7-d6 |

"Me too".

| 6 | Bc1-e3 | ... |

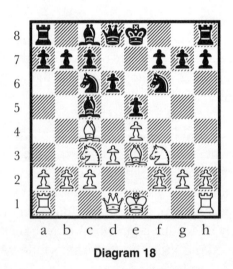

Diagram 18

A move with some bite. White opposes Bishops, thus cancelling the Black Bishop's attack on the f2-square. In addition, White is hoping Black will exchange with Bc5xe3, after which White will play f2xe3.

Diagram 19

In this position, the two White pawns on e3 and e4 control all of the vital central squares, making it impossible for Black to place his Knights anywhere useful. In addition, White will Castle King-side, placing his Rook on the f-file, which is now a half-open file (open from White's side of the board, but not from Black's).

By maneuvering his pieces to the King-side, White will be able to organize an attack down this file.

| 6 | ... | Bc5-b6 |

Black sees the danger and sidesteps it by retreating his Bishop.

| 7 | Qd1-d2 | ... |

Gets the Queen off the back rank.

7	...	Bc8-e6

Black has the same plan as White.

8	Bc4-b5	...

White avoids exchanging Bishops and instead pins the Knight to Black's King.

8	...	0-0

Black breaks the pin by castling.

9	d3-d4	...

White tries to grab more space in the center. If he delays this advance, Black will play d6-d5 himself and take the initiative.

9	...	e5xd4

Black knows the resulting exchanges will free his game.

10	Nf3xd4	Nc6xd4
11	Be3xd4	Bb6xd4
12	Qd2xd4	d6-d5

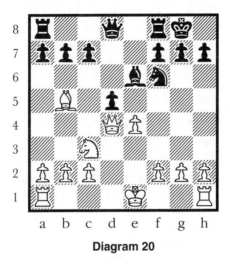

Diagram 20

Black has achieved a completely equal game. A possible continuation from here is:

13	e4xd5	Nf6xd5
14	Nc3xd5	Qd8xd5
15	Qd4xd5	Be6xd5

Black has no problems in this position. White will have to safeguard his King, perhaps with f2-f3 and Ke1-f2 (with so few pieces left on the board, there is no reason for the King to hide in the corner any longer). Both sides will bring their Rooks to the central squares, on d1 and e1 for White, d8 and e8 for Black. More trades will result, since neither side will want to concede the central files to the other. Building up an advantage will be difficult for either side.

There's an important lesson to be learned here. Simply developing your pieces to good squares in the opening is not enough to guarantee you an advantage later on. If your opponent knows enough to do the same, the game may quickly peter out into a sterile equality. It's necessary to play with imagination in order to inject dynamic tension into a position.

EVANS GAMBIT

Chess openings are named after all sorts of things - countries, cities, tournaments, pieces, rich benefactors - so it's always refreshing to find one, like the **Evans Gambit**, that's named after its inventor. Captain Evans was a British military man of the early nineteenth century.

The story goes that he was only an average player of his time, but one day he discovered and started to analyze a new gambit which seemed to him quite promising. After some months of study in 1838, he was able one day to spring his new weapon on none other than the best English player of his time - MacDonnell. The result was a crushing victory for Captain Evans and his new gambit.

The gambit remained popular for many years, and it was a favorite of the American chess genius Paul Morphy during his brief, incandescent career. By the end of the century it had faded in popularity somewhat, although it still occasionally appears in master practice.

The Evans Gambit is for players who like open lines, bold attacks, and exciting piece play at the cost of a pawn. White's attacking chances are about as good as in the Danish Gambit, at the cost of slightly less material.

As in the Danish Gambit, White's attack needs to crash through quickly; if Black survives to the endgame, his extra pawn may win for him.

	White:	**Black:**
1	e2-e4	e7-e5
2	Ng1-f3	Nb8-c6
3	Bf1-c4	Bf8-c5
4	b2-b4!	

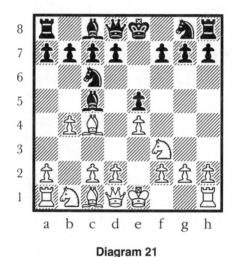

Diagram 21

White's fourth move, b2-b4, is the key move in the Evans Gambit. The idea is to lure Black's Bishop to the b4 square at the cost of a pawn. White can then play c2-c3 attacking the Bishop and also preparing d2-d4 with a strong pawn center.

It's a daring idea that typically leads to wild and exciting play.

MORPHY VS. SHULTEN

To get a flavor for the Evans Gambit, let's follow the course of a game between Paul Morphy and J.W. Schulten, an American amateur of Morphy's time. The game was played in New York in 1857, just prior to Morphy's victory in the First American Chess Congress. We continue from the last diagram, with Morphy having White.

4	...	Bc5xb4

Black can decline the gambit with Bc5-b6, but that leads to complicated play which is only marginally less scary than in the main variations. So Black figures he might as well have a pawn for his troubles.

5	c2-c3	Bb4-c5
6	0-0	...

Morphy plans to play d2-d4 next turn. He knows Black can't prevent the move, so he first takes time to safeguard his King and activate the Rook.

6	...	d7-d6

Black prepares to develop his Bishop on c8.

7	d2-d4	e5xd4
8	c3xd4	Bc5-b6

42

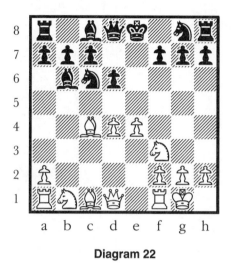

Diagram 22

This is the **Normal Variation** of the Evans, which has busied theoreticians for over 150 years! White has a better center and more active play; Black has an extra pawn.

9	d4-d5

Morphy's favorite attacking maneuver. Another move, leading to different complications, is Nb1-c3.

9	...	Nc6-e7

On this square the Knight tends to get in the way of Black's other pieces. Later it was discovered that Nc6-a5 was more effective.

10	e4-e5!

Morphy had a great genius for dynamic play in open positions. This move prepares to open the e-file leading to Black's King, as well as make it more difficult for Black to develop his Knight on g8.

10	...	Bc8-g4
11	h2-h3	

Morphy sacrifices another pawn to open more lines for his pieces.

11	...	Bg4xf3
12	Qd1xf3	Bb6-d4

The double attack on the Rook on a1 and the pawn on e5 will win the pawn; but Morphy has foreseen this.

13	Nb1-c3	Bd4xe5
14	Bc4-b5 check!	

This move prevents Black from castling.

14	...	Ke8-f8

Diagram 23

Although two pawns down, White has a great advantage in space and piece activity. Black's King is uncomfortable on f8 and he will have difficulty developing his King's Rook. Morphy excelled in handling such positions.

15   Bc1-b2

Guards the Knight and thereby frees the Queen for activity.

15   ...   c7-c6?

A typical defensive error. Black is trying to beat off the attack but instead just drives White's Bishop to a more useful square. A better defensive plan was Ne7-g6 and then Qd8-f6, untangling his pieces and contesting the center.

16   Bb5-d3   Ng8-f6
17   Ra1-e1

Morphy sees the threat to his pawn on d5 but does not waste time defending it. Instead he brings yet another piece to the attack.

17   ...   Be5xc3?

A big mistake. Black exchanges off his best defensive piece for White's pinned Knight at c3. Although he will win another pawn, he will soon be helpless against the coordinated attack of the White pieces.

18	Bb2xc3	Nf6xd5
19	Bc3-a1	

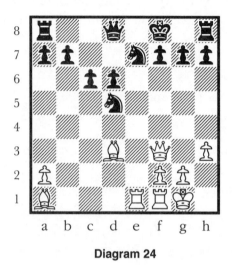

Diagram 24

Morphy puts the Bishop well out of harm's way. Notice how his pieces sweep the board, while Black's men are mostly huddled on the first rank.

19	...	f7-f6?

Not a good idea. Black is trying to neutralize the power of White's Bishop on a1, as well as give his King a square for moving off the first rank. Black probably imagines that he'll continue with something like Kf8-f7, Rh8-e8, and Ne7-g6, untangling his ragtag army and contesting the center.

But Morphy's not about to allow that! Every pawn move around the King loosens the defensive structure, and Morphy is quick to take advantage of the fact that the e6 square is no longer defended by a Black pawn.

20	**Re1-e6!**	**Qd8-d7**

The Queen tries to drive away the Rook.

21	**Rf1-e1!**

"No thanks" says Morphy. Suddenly White has amassed considerable power on the open e-file. He also has a big threat, which Black overlooks.

21	**...**	**b7-b5?**

Irrelevant. The action is over on the other side of the board. Now Morphy uncorks the fireworks.

22	**Re6xe7!**	**Nd5xe7**
23	**Ba1xf6!**	

One sacrifice follows another. If Black now takes the Bishop, Morphy would reply with Qf3xf6 check. Then Kf8-g8 would allow Re1xe7, winning, while Kf8-e8 allows Qf6xh8 check, with the same result.

23	**...**	**Ne7-d5**
24	**Bf6-e7 double check!**	

Black's King is in check from both the Queen and the Bishop. A double check can only be answered by moving the King.

24	**...**	**Kf8-g8**
25	**Bd3-f5!**	

Diagram 25

An elegant finish. Morphy attacks the Queen and in addition threatens Bf5-e6 check, either mating or winning the Black Queen. Schulten gives up.

THE KING'S GAMBIT

The **King's Gambit** was the workhorse opening for attacking players throughout the 19th century. It begins with these moves:

	White:	Black:
1	e2-e4	e7-e5
2	f2-f4	

Diagram 26

The idea behind the King's Gambit is very simple. White is offering a pawn to lure Black into giving up the center. After Black plays e5xf4, White will eventually follow up with d2-d4, grabbing complete central control. He will develop his King's Knight to f3, his King's Bishop to c4, and castle King-side, bringing his King's Rook to the half-open f-file. The Rook, Bishop, and Knight will eventually mount an attack on Black's weak f7-square. Of course, Black gets to make some moves in the meanwhile, but that's the general idea.

The King's Gambit is an excellent choice for players who like unbalanced, wide-open positions with dangerous attacking chances for both sides. Often White is able to regain his gambit pawn and still retain a healthy initiative.

Like many of the open games, the King's Gambit is seen less these days than formerly, but it's still a dangerous weapon in the hands of a skilled attacking player. In recent years both Boris Spassky and Bobby Fischer have used the opening to score smashing victories. It's double-edged and dangerous, and guaranteed to lead to exciting play.

SPASSKY VS. BRONSTEIN

For a sample of the King's Gambit's bite, I've selected one of the most brilliant games from the last fifty years, a battle between the Russian grandmasters Boris Spassky and David Bronstein in the 1959 Soviet Championship
.

Spassky was a youngster of 23 when the game was played, but seven years later he would win the World Championship. The game was so famous at the time that in 1963 the producers of the James Bond film From Russia with Love used the position after move 21 for the conclusion of the game between grandmasters Kronsteen and MacAdams that starts the movie.

	White (Spassky)	Black (Bronstein)
1	e2-e4	e7-e5
2	f2-f4	e5xf4

Black can decline the gambit in various ways, but there's no reason not to accept it.

3	Ng1-f3

This is the most popular third move, which prevents Black from playing Qd8-h4 check. Another way of playing is Bf1-c4, the **King's Bishop's Gambit**, which Bobby Fischer once used to defeat Larry Evans.

| 3 | ... | d7-d5 |

As we've seen in some other openings, this is a key freeing move for Black. Many other moves have been played here, however, including g7-g5, d7-d6, Ng8-f6, and Bf8-e7. Take your choice. For the record, the most analyzed and played move here is g7-g5.

| 4 | e4xd5 | Bf8-d6 |

A bit more usual is Ng8-f6. The purpose of this move is to protect the pawn on f4 while later playing Ng8-e7-g6.

5	Nb1-c3	Ng8-e7
6	d2-d4	0-0
7	Bf1-d3	Nb8-d7

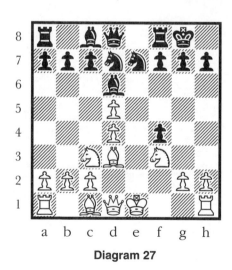

Diagram 27

There's nothing mysterious about the last few moves on both sides. Each player is developing his pieces to the most active squares available. Although Black's position looks a little cramped, he should be able to complete his development by Nd7-f6 and Ne7-g6. Or so it seems.

8	0-0	h7-h6

This last move was questioned by analysts after the game, with good reason. Black wastes a move and weakens his King-side, making it easier for White to get an attack going later. The purpose is to support a later g7-g5, protecting the pawn on f4, but Black doesn't have the time for such a plan. In open games, *time* and *development* are crucially important. Black usually can't afford to lose time without running the risk of being overrun. Better was Nd7-f6, as mentioned in the last note.

9	Nc3-e4

White surrenders the pawn on d5 (which was hard to hold in the long run) to move his pieces towards the King-side.

9	...	Ne7xd5
10	c2-c4	

Grabbing central space *with a tempo* (a chess expression for gaining a move).

10	...	Nd5-e3

Retreating the Knight allows White to play c4-c5 with a big advantage in space.

11	Bc1xe3	f4xe3

12	c4-c5	Bd6-e7

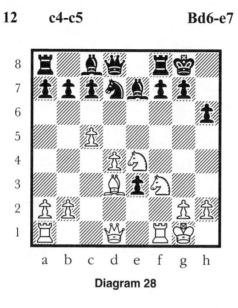

Diagram 28

13	Bd3-c2!

A grandmaster move! A lesser player might have continued with Qd1-e2, trying to capture the Black pawn as quickly as possible. Spassky figures the pawn will take care of itself later, and instead asks how he can best arrange his pieces for an upcoming attack on the Black King. He sees that by putting the Bishop on c2 and the Queen on d3, he opens up possibilities of eventually getting the Queen to h7 with checkmating threats. This sort of move is difficult to find over the board and distinguishes the top grandmaster from the merely talented amateur.

13	...	Rf8-e8

A move which both defends and develops. The Rook rates to be more active on the open e-file than on the closed f-file, and the move also frees the way for the Knight to move to f8, defending the crucial h7 square.

14   Qd1-d3!

The Queen lines up on the diagonal with the Bishop, creating what's called a **battery**. White now threatens to move the Knight on e4, clearing the way for the Queen to go to h7 with check, and then to h8 with mate. The Queen also attacks the loose pawn at e3, but that's insignificant in light of the more serious threats.

14   ...   e3-e2

Since this pawn will be lost eventually anyway, Black voluntarily gives it away to induce White to move his Queen off the b1-h7 diagonal. After White plays Qd3xe2, he reasons, Black can defend with Nd7-f8, creating a secure fortress, then develop the Bishop on c8 to e6, f5, or g4 as circumstances warrant. It's a good plan, but unfortunately White now uncorks one of the most brilliant moves ever seen on a chess board, and Black's situation takes a turn for the worse.

Diagram 29

15   Ne4-d6!!

Amazing. White allows his Rook to be taken **with check**, rather than lose a move retreating his Queen. He realizes that Black's position is temporarily disorganized, but if Black is allowed one extra move (for instance Nd7-f8) his game will quickly come together. So White strikes now, investing a Rook in the process. His immediate threat is Qd3-h7 check, Kg8-f8, Qh7-h8 mate.

15   ...   Nd7-f8

Taking the Rook this turn would transpose into the game position after two more moves. Black needs to guard the h7 square against the Queen's invasion in any event.

16   Nd6xf7!!

White blasts open the Black King's defenses from another direction.

16   ...   e2xf1 check

Why not? It's free, and White's attack is no less powerful in any event.

17   Ra1xf1

Diagram 30

17	...	Bc8-f5

Black voluntarily gives back a Bishop to gain a tempo and break (he hopes) the force of White's attack. Why didn't he take White's Knight on f7? Let's look and see the amazing finish Spassky had prepared when he made his 15th move.

If Black had taken the Knight with 17... Kg8xf7, White would have responded with 18 Nf3-e5 double check! A double check can only be answered by a King move, so Black would retreat with 18... Kf7-g8. White would then play the real point of the combination: 19 Qd3-h7 check!! Black would be forced to capture: 19... Nf8xh7. And White would cap his brilliant play with 20 Bc2-b3 check Kg8-h8 21 Ne5-g6 checkmate! An incredible finish. Remember that White had to foresee all this before playing his 15th move.

18   Qd3xf5

Now White has a Bishop and a pawn for his lost Rook, and the attack besides. He should win easily.

18   ...   Qd8-d7

Here's the point of Black's Bishop sacrifice. He's able to develop the Queen and gain a move by offering to exchange Queens. Black hopes that this gain of time will let him beat off the attack.

19   Qf5-f4   Be7-f6

Black looks like he may be getting out of trouble. But Spassky still has plenty of attacking chances left.

20   Nf3-e5!   Qd7-e7

If Black plays 20... Bf6xe5, White replies with 21 Nf7xe5 and his attack will continue.

21   Bc2-b3!

This was the starting point for the Kronsteen-MacAdams game in *From Russia with Love*, although in the movie version the White pawns on c5 and d4 were omitted. The actor who played Comrade Kronsteen, by the way, bore an uncanny resemblance to Anatoly Karpov, who became World Champion in 1975, twelve years after the movie was made.

21   ...   Bf6xe5

| 22 | Nf7xe5 discovered check | Kg8-h7 |

If 22... Kg8-h8, White wins with 23 Qf4-g3! threatening both Rf1-f7 and Rf1xf8 check.

| 23 | Qf4-e4 check! | Black resigns |

If Black plays Kh7-h8, White wins with Rf1xf8 check and Ne5-g6 check. If Black defends with g7-g6, then Rf1-f7 check wins. A marvelous game.

FOUR KNIGHTS GAME

The **Four Knight Game** begins with both sides developing their Knights:

1	e2-e4	e7-e5
2	Ng1-f3	Nb8-c6
3	Nb1-c3	Ng8-f6

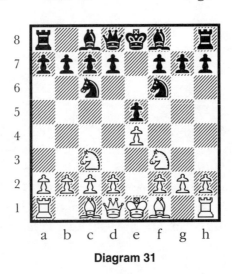

Diagram 31

Once White's main choice when playing e2-e4, it's

now rarely seen on the grandmaster circuit. However, it can be a useful weapon at the amateur level. The **Four Knight's Game** is a good choice if you want a closed game with slow but steady pressure on Black's position. You won't generate the exciting attacks characteristic of the gambit openings we've looked at, but you won't need to sacrifice material either.

We'll follow the main line for a few moves to give you a flavor of the way the game can develop.

4	**Bf1-b5**

The most aggressive post for the Bishop.

4	**...**	**Bf8-b4**

Black continues to play symmetrically. A word of caution is in order here. Many beginners think that by copying their opponent's move, they can automatically frustrate his intentions. That's not really true.

If both sides play the same moves, White will eventually reach a point where he can break the symmetry with a threat, and achieve a substantial advantage. Black must be careful to break the symmetry himself before that happens.

5	**0-0**	**0-0**
6	**d2-d3**	**Bb4xc3**

Black breaks the symmetry himself to saddle White with doubled pawns.

7	b2xc3	d7-d6
8	Bc1-g5	

This pin gives White the best chance for an advantage.

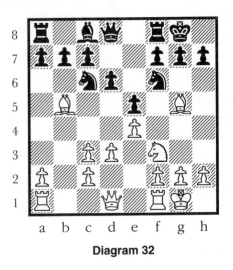

Diagram 32

8	...	Qd8-e7!

This maneuver, Queen to e7 followed by the Knight from c6 to d8 to e6, is known as the **Metzger Unpin**. The point of the maneuver is to relieve the pressure from the White Bishops, and it's a reliable method for Black to achieve equality.

9	Rf1-e1	Nc6-d8
10	d3-d4	Bc8-g4

This move will eventually lead to further simplification, which will further ease Black's problems.

11	h2-h3

Chases away the Bishop, but at a cost of weakening his
King-side pawns.

11	...	Bg4-h5
12	g2-g4	Bh5-g6
13	d4-d5	

White has an advantage in space but there's little he can
do with it.

13	...	c7-c6
14	Bb5-f1	Ra8-c8
15	c3-c4	b7-b6

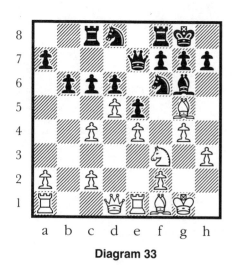

Diagram 33

The game is about even. White should try to mount an
attack on the Queen-side, where he has more space, with
moves like Qd1-d2, a2-a4, and a4-a5. Black can counter
by moving his Knight from d8 to b7 to c5, where it adds
to the pressure on White's e4-pawn.

THE VIENNA GAME

The **Vienna Game** is for players who want a slightly offbeat approach to the double King pawn openings. It features active attacking chances along the f-file, usually without the necessity of sacrificing material as in the other gambit openings.

The Vienna Game is characterized by the move 2 Nb1-c3 (after 1 e2-e4 e7-e5). The strategic idea is straightforward: White wants to play Bf1-c4, d2-d3, and f2-f4. This lets him advance his f-pawn without risking the complications of the King's Gambit.

Later on, he can play Ng1-f3, 0-0, and perhaps build up an attack down the f-file.

It's a good plan, and if Black plays passively, White can build up a strong attack. Black needs to play actively to counteract these plans. Experience has shown that he can usually equalize against the Vienna game, although he may need to thread his way through some hair-raising complications.

1	e2-e4	e7-e5
2	Nb1-c3	

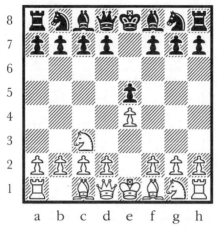

Diagram 34

The characteristic move of the **Vienna Game**.

2	...	Ng8-f6

Black's most active response. This involves a tactical trick, as we shall see.

3	Bf1-c4	Nf6xe4!

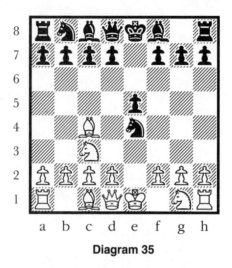

Diagram 35

Black's point! He's not really sacrificing a Knight, since if White captures with Nc3xe4, Black can win his piece back with d7-d5! (This maneuver is known as the **fork trick**, and it's an equalizing strategy for Black in many openings.)

The real idea is to eliminate White's central pawn, while at the same time simplifying the game by trading a few pieces. However, White has ways to keep the game complicated.

4	Qd1-h5!	

A powerful move which threatens both Qh5xe5 check and Qh5xf7 mate!

4	...	Ne4-d6!

An excellent, multi-purpose response. The Knight moves back to safety and simultaneously guards the pawn on f7 and attacks the Bishop on c4. Although the pawn on e5 is left unprotected, White doesn't really want to take it. Why? Because Black would respond to Qh5xe5 check with Qd8-e7, pinning White's Queen against his King and forcing an exchange of Queens.

That would lead to a very drawish position, and White is trying to get an advantage.

5   Bc4-b3

Safeties the Bishop and keeps up the pressure on f7.

5   ...   Nb8-c6

Develops the Knight and guards the pawn on e5.

6   d2-d4!?

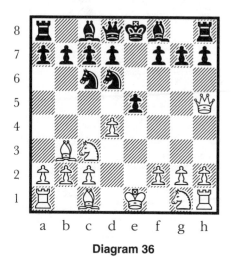

Diagram 36

This is the **Adams Gambit**, named after Weaver Adams, a somewhat eccentric American master of the 1940s and 1950s, who popularized it. The idea is to sacrifice another pawn for open lines and quick development.

| 6 | ... | Nc6xd4 |
| 7 | Nc3-d5 | |

To prevent Black from playing his Queen to e7. Now White really threatens Qh5xe5 check.

| 7 | ... | Nd4-e6 |
| 8 | Qh5xe5 | c7-c6! |

Chases away the annoying Knight and prepares for some simplification.

| 9 | Nd5-f4 | Qd8-e7 |
| 10 | Ng1-f3 | Nd6-f5! |

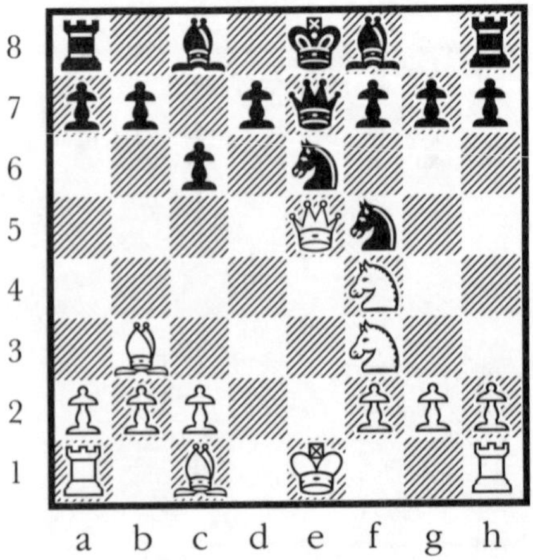

Diagram 37

Black responds with some ingenuity of his own. Notice that White can't take the Knight: if he plays 11 Qe5xf5, Black responds with Ne6-d4 discovered check, attacking White's King with his Queen and White's Queen with his Knight. White can save both for a turn with Qf5-e5, but then Black plays Nd4xf3 check, followed by Queen takes Queen.

| 11 | 0-0 | Ne6-d4 |

Since Black is a pawn ahead, his defensive job will be simplified if he can exchange White's dangerous Queen. Although White isn't eager to exchange, his Queen has no other convenient move.

12	Qe5xe7 check	Bf8xe7
13	Nf3xd4	Nf5xd4
14	Rf1-e1	Nd4-e6
15	Nf4-d3	

Again, exchanging pieces makes life easier for Black. However, White's attack is running out of steam.

| 15 | ... | 0-0 |
| 16 | f2-f4 | Be7-f6 |

Black has a sound extra pawn, with good chances in the endgame. Black will attempt to free his game by playing d7-d5, Bc8-d7, and Rf8-e8. White will attempt to open up the position for his better-developed pieces with pawn thrusts like c2-c4 and g2-g4-g5, while developing his Bishop at d2 and his other Rook at d1. Black's extra pawn means that he will do well in any endgame; thus, White must try to win in the middle game.

5

THE RUY LOPEZ

*The **Ruy Lopez**,* named for a Spanish cleric who was considered the strongest player in the world during the 16th century, is currently most popular of the double King pawn openings.

The reason for this can be summed up in one word - pressure!

FIRST WORD

The Ruy Lopez is the opening to play if you want to start preparing for the day when you'll be competing in master-level events.

We'll take a look at this exciting opening now!

The play is tricky and intricate, but Black will have a more difficult time attaining equality than against any other King-pawn opening.

The **Ruy Lopez** starts with these three moves:

1	e2-e4	e7-e5
2	Ng1-f3	Nb8-c6
3	Bf1-b5!	

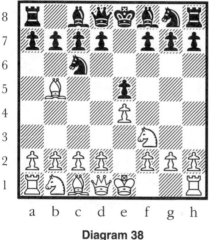

Diagram 38

White's second move, Ng1-f3, attacked the Black pawn at e5. Black defended this pawn by moving a Knight to c6. White's third move, Bf1-b5, attacks this defender.

This sets up a chain reaction: White threatens, now or in the future, to capture the Black Knight with his Bishop, thereby eliminating the defender of the e5-pawn and leaving the pawn vulnerable.

It's not a real threat yet. The reason is that even if Black didn't make a move and White continued with 4 Bb5xc6 d7xc6 5 Nf3xe5, Black could regain his pawn with the tactical shot Qd8-d4!, attacking the undefended White Knight and the undefended pawn on e4.

But even though it's not a threat now, it may become a real threat in the near future, and Black must continually be alert to threats against the e5-pawn.

These latent threats are the source of White's continuing pressure in the opening.

As we've seen, in many of the other double-King-pawn openings, Black is able to equalize by playing an opportune d7-d5, liquidating some central pawns and dissolving the tension.

In the Ruy Lopez, that central thrust is much harder to achieve, since Black usually has to keep his d-pawn at d6 to guard the e5-pawn. White usually builds up an early advantage in space and keeps it well into the middle game or even the ending.

Let's look at a couple of Ruy Lopez games and get a flavor of this fascinating opening.

We'll start with a game of the great Bobby Fischer, known throughout his career as a great virtuoso of the White side of the Ruy Lopez. The game was played in the 1963-64 U.S. Championship, when Fischer (age 20) was in the process of winning his sixth straight national title.

FISCHER VS. WEINSTEIN

	White (Fischer)	Black (Weinstein)
1	e2-e4	e7-e5
2	Ng1-f3	Nb8-c6
3	Bf1-b5	a7-a6

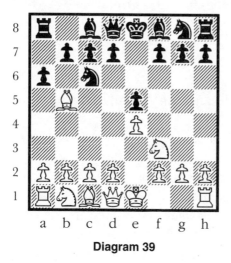

Diagram 39

This pawn push is the most popular way of meeting the Ruy Lopez. It's known as the **Morphy Defense** (after the nineteenth-century American genius, Paul Morphy) and it's really a sophisticated way of defending the e-pawn. The idea is that since White can't immediately win the e-pawn by capturing the Knight, he'll instead retreat the Bishop to a4. Then Black will be able, if needed, to later save his Knight from capture by playing b7-b5 at an opportune time.

4   Bb5-a4

This retreat isn't forced. White could also play Bb5xc6, the **Exchange Variation**, which Fischer himself used to score many impressive victories later in his career. But the retreat, maintaining the attack on the Knight, is the most common move.

4   ...   Ng8-f6

Black develops his King's Knight and attacks the White e-pawn.

5   0-0

White castles, ignoring the attack on his e-pawn.

5   ...   Bf8-e7

Black could also take the e-pawn with Nf6xe4. That's known as the **Open Variation**, and it leads to an exciting and complicated game. White always wins his pawn back, starting with 6 d2-d4, and usually gets a slightly advantage. Some players of the Black pieces prefer the positions that result, while other players generally like Bf8-e7. It's mostly a matter of taste.

6   Rf1-e1

White guards the King pawn with his Rook. Now that the e-pawn is firmly guarded, White finally has a real threat of 7 Ba4xc6 d7xc6 8 Nf3xe5, winning a pawn. Black must find a way to guard his e-pawn again.

6   ...   b7-b5

The point of a7-a6: this move is now possible and eliminates the Bishop's attack on the Knight.

7   Ba4-b3

The Bishop retreats but to a more active square, where it attacks the d5 square (preventing the freeing move d7-d5).

7	...	d7-d6

Since Black can't play d7-d5 without eventually losing his e-pawn (White would play e4xd5 followed by Nf3xe5), he settles for shoring up his central pawn, thus freeing the Knight on c6 for other duties. In addition, the Bishop on c8 now has more possibilities for active play.

8	c2-c3

An important move with two purposes. First, the pawn supports a later d2-d4 by White, establishing his long-run goal: two pawns abreast in the center at d4 and e4. If Black were to then exchange pawns by e5xd4, White will be able to recapture *with a pawn*, by c3xd4, maintaining his pawn center.

The second purpose of the move is to provide a flight square for the White-squared Bishop at c2. If Black later plays nc6-a4, trying to exchange his Knight for the Bishop, White will be able to keep his Bishop on the board by playing Bb3-c2.

You might well ask: "Why all this fuss about preserving a Bishop? Isn't a Bishop just as valuable as a Knight?" Not always, it turns out. In the Ruy Lopez, experience has shown that the white-squared Bishop is particularly valuable, guarding squares like d5 and e6, while sometimes later on participating in an attack against the Black King at f7 and h7. So White is usually careful to maintain this Bishop as long as possible.

8	...	0-0

Black safeties the King and gets the Rook closer to the center.

9	h2-h3

A quiet move which nonetheless has a profound bearing on the struggle to control the center squares.

White wants to play d2-d4, at which point the pawn on d4 would be guarded three ways: by the pawn on c3, the Knight on f3, and the Queen on d1. But if Black then played Bc8-g4, his Bishop would pin the Knight on f3 against the Queen and threaten to capture it.

If White recaptured with the Queen, two of the defenders of d4 would have been removed with one stroke. To circumvent this sequence, White first prevents the Bishop's move to g4.

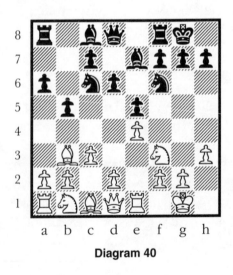

Diagram 40

This position has occurred thousands of times in master and grandmaster-level chess over the past century. White has a small but enduring advantage, based on his ability to construct and maintain a pawn center at d4 and e4. White's last several moves have been played with an eye to providing a stable foundation to that center, and he's now ready to play d2-d4.

Black has tried many moves in this position over the years, including Nc6-a5, Nc6-b8, Bc8-b7, Bc8-e6, Nf6-d7, h7-h6, and Rf8-e8. All give Black reasonable play, but none has been definitely shown to equalize. In this game, Weinstein played

9   ...   Nc6-a5

This was the most popular move from the turn of the century up until the 1960s. Lately, it has been superceded in popularity by some of the other lines. Black's idea is to get some elbow room for his pieces by playing c7-c5 and Qd8-c7.

10   Bb3-c2

White retreats to preserve his valuable Bishop for later action. It's a sound strategic principle that the side that is cramped for space (in this case Black) tries to exchange pieces, while the side with an advantage in space (White) avoids exchanges when practicable.

10   ...   c7-c5
11   d2-d4

Diagram 41

At last! White finally achieves the strong pawn center that he has been maneuvering toward from move 3. His move also contains a direct threat: capturing twice on e5, winning the e-pawn.

How should Black respond?

Two approaches are possible. The first is the so-called **Strong-Point Variation**, where Black allows White to keep his pawn center but tries to equalize by maintaining his own central pawn on e5. This involves leaving the pawn structure as is but defending e5 with moves like Qd8-c7, Na5-c6, Rf8-e8, and Be7-f8. Black's idea is that White will have difficulty in translating his space advantage into anything concrete as long as Black can maintain a strong pawn on e5.

The second approach, which Weinstein adopts in this game, is to exchange pawns with c5xd4, opening the c-file, then use the open file for counterplay against White's position. This leads to sharper and more open play than in the first variation, and is often favored by players who like fluid and tactical positions.

The danger is that White, with his greater command of space, may be able to use the c-file for his own purposes.

| 11 | ... | c5xd4 |
| 12 | c3xd4 | Bc8-b7! |

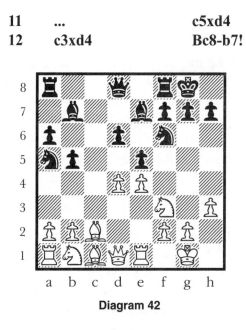

Diagram 42

An ingenious move which offers a temporary sacrifice of a pawn. If White captures Black's e-pawn with 13 d4xe5 d6xe5 14 Nf3xe5, Black will equalize with 14... Qd8xd1 15 Re1xd1 Bb7xe4, winning back the pawn. With all the center pawns eliminated, Black will have equalized the game. Instead Fischer plays

| 13 | d4-d5! |

Closing the center and establishing a real advantage in space.

| 13 | ... | Bb7-c8 |

Black's last maneuver (Bc8-b7-c8) might look silly but in fact has a real point. Black would rather play the position with White's pawn on d5 rather than d4. As long as the pawn was on d4, Black had to be constantly alert to threats against his e-pawn.

With the pawn structure now **fixed,** no exchanges possible, these threats are gone and Black can try to maneuver his pieces to the best available squares. With that in mind, the Bishop serves no purpose on b7, but will be quite useful on d7, where it will support the pawn on b5 and keep the b-file open for Black's Queen and Rooks.

| 14 | Nb1-d2 |

The Knight develops to a square where it guards c4. White wants to continue with b2-b4, driving back Black's Knight, without allowing the Knight to go to c4. The temporary congestion in White's position is of no concern; Black can't exploit it and White's pieces will quickly regroup to new squares.

| 14 | ... | g7-g6 |

To prevent White from moving a Knight to f5 after a maneuver like Nd2-f1-e3.

| 15 | b2-b4! |

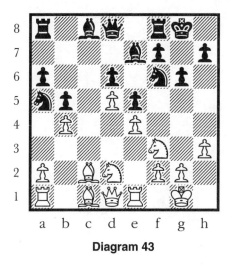

Diagram 43

White begins to expand on the Queenside. Watch how quickly White's pieces now assume active positions.

15	...	Na5-b7
16	a2-a4!	Bc8-d7
17	a4xb5	a6xb5

A mistake, which leaves Black's Knight on b7 with no place to go. A better plan was Bd7xb5, followed by a6-a5, gaining some freedom.

| 18 | Ra1xa8 | Qd8xa8 |
| 19 | Re1-e3! | |

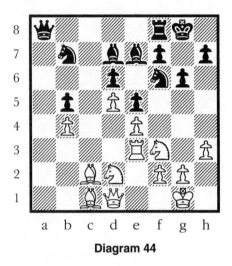

Diagram 44

A fine idea. White plans to swing the Rook over to a3, where it will chase away Black's Queen and control the now open a-file. *Rooks belong on open files* is a well-known chess maxim. Sometimes it takes considerable ingenuity to see how to get them there. Fischer was never lacking in this regard.

19   ...   Qa8-c8

Black can't prevent White from moving the Rook to a3, so he reposition the Queen along the potentially useful c-file.

20   Re3-a3

White's Rook grabs the open file and prepares to penetrate via a7 or a6.

20   ...   Qc8-c7

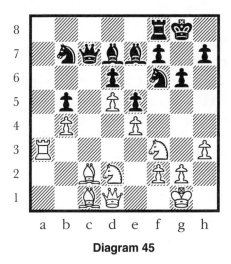

Diagram 45

Black's Queen moves off the back rank, thus allowing the Rook to get into play. Notice how little scope Black's pieces have in this position: the Knight on b7 can only retreat to d8, the Bishop on d7 has an unappetizing choice between retreating to c8 or e8, the Bishop on e7 can only move back to d8, the Rook is reduced to crawling along the back rank, and the Knight at f6 can only move to the side of the board at h5 or back to e8.

In fact, of Black's six pieces other than the King, only two have safe moves to squares beyond Black's first rank! Watch how Fischer exploits this lack of mobility over the next few moves to control the whole board.

21   Nd2-b3

There is no hurry about penetrating with the Rook. First White moves the Knight to an ideal square, preparing to develop the Bishop to either e3 or g5, as appropriate.

21   ...   Nf6-h5

A move with a couple of possibilities. The Knight might go to f4, or back to g7 with the idea of supporting the thrust f7-f5, gaining some space on the Kingside. Since White has a firm grip on the center and the Queenside, Black needs to generate some counterplay elsewhere.

22   Bc2-b3   ...

The White-squared Bishop moves to a more active square, attacking the pawn on b5.

22   ...   Rf8-c8

It's not clear what Black hopes to accomplish with this move, since he's not going to be able to penetrate into White's position via the c-file. Nh5-g7 looks a little better.

23   Qd1-f1!

A hard move to find, but very effective. White attacks the b-pawn a second time, and Black suddenly can't defend it (Qc7-b6 fails to Bc1-e3, chasing away the Queen).

23   ...   Nh5-f6

Black does the best he can. The Knight attacks the e4-pawn, so that after 24 Bd3xb5 Black can respond with Nf6xe4.

24   Bc1-g5

The Bishop springs into play by attacking the Knight on

f6 and pinning it to the undefended Bishop on e7. White again threatens to capture on b5.

24   **...**   **Rc8-b8**

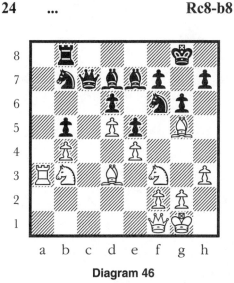

Diagram 46

Another clever moves which guards the b-pawn by means of a hidden trap. If Fischer now captures the pawn by 25 Bd3xb5 Bd7xb5 26 Qf1xb5, Black will play Nb7-c5!, uncovering an attack on the Queen by the Rook. White will retreat his Queen, and Black will continue with Nc5xe4, winning back the pawn with an advantageous position. Fischer sees this, of course, and continues with his plan to tie Black in knots.

25   **Ra3-a7!**

The Rook penetrates into Black's position, incidentally pinning the Knight to the Queen.

25   **...**   **Qc7-d8**

Unpins the Knight on b7 and protects the Bishop on e7, thereby unpinning the other Knight as well. Quite a lot to accomplish with just one little move!

26   Qf1-a1

White brings up the heavy artillery. Now the Queen is poised to move into Black's position at a6.

26   ...   Qd8-e8

Black can't stop the Queen's penetration.

27   Qa1-a6

Attacks the Knight at b7 twice, threatening to capture it with the Rook.

27   ...   Qe8-c8

Guards the Knight a second time.

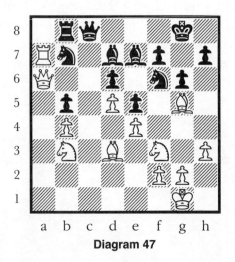

Diagram 47

Fischer has artfully used his space advantage to maneuver all his pieces to active positions. Black, however, seems to have guarded everything for now. How does White break through?

28   Nf3xe5!

This ingenious shot causes Black's position to crumble. Notice that the play works because White's Queen, from a6, will attack the Black Knight on f6 once the Black d-pawn moves.

28	...	d6xe5
29	Bg5xf6	Be7xf6
30	Qa6xf6	Qc8-c3

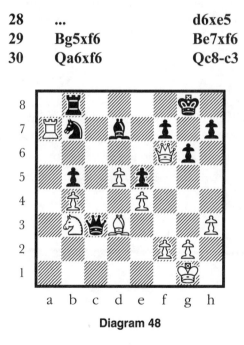

Diagram 48

White has won a pawn, but Black seems finally to have some counterplay. The Queen breaks into White's position and threatens two pieces.

31   Nb3-c5!

The Knight moves to guard the Bishop, while at the same time attacking Black's Knight and Bishop.

31   ...   Nb7xc5

Black has no choice.

32   b4xc5

Now White threatens Ra7xd7 followed by Qf6xf7 check and a quick checkmate. Black again has no choice.

32   ...   Bd7-e8
33   Bd3-f1   Qc3xc5

Although Black has won back his pawn, White has a tremendous advantage by virtue of his passed d-pawn and his potential attack on the Black King's position. In addition, the Black e-pawn can't be defended.

34   Ra7-e7

Guards the Rook, attacks the e-pawn, and prepares to move the pawn to d6 and d7.

34   ...   b5-b4

Black has a passed pawn of his own.

35   d5-d6

White ignores the e-pawn for the moment and threatens d6-d7 winning the Bishop.

35	...	Qc5-b6
36	Bf1-c4	

The Bishop finally joins the attack with a decisive threat: 37 Bc4xf7 check, Be8xf7 38 Qf6xf7 check Kg8-h8 39 Qf7-g7 mate. At this point Black's allotted time elapsed, but he had no defense in any case.

Notice how Fischer used the entire board for his ideas: first, an advantage in space leading to an invasion on the Queenside; next, a breakthrough in the center; and finally, a decisive attack on the Kingside. Black, with his cramped position, couldn't organize his pieces for defense.

JUNHKE VS. KARPOV

In our previous game, a few slight inaccuracies resulted in Black's being enveloped, squeezed, and crushed. Now let's take a look at Black's possibilities in the hands of a master of defense: Anatoly Karpov, World Champion from 1975 to 1985. This next game was played in the World Junior Championship in 1969, won by Karpov with a scintillating score of 10-1. White is played by Jurgen Junhke.

	White (Junhke)	Black (Karpov)
1	e2-e4	e7-e5
2	Ng1-f3	Nb8-c6
3	Bf1-b5	a7-a6
4	Bb5-a4	Ng8-f6

So far, the same as the previous game. Instead of Fischer's 5 0-0 leading to slow but steady pressure, however, Junhke tries a different move, attempting to open the game quickly.

5   d2-d4!?

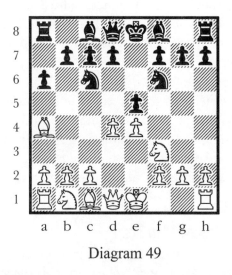

Diagram 49

White launches an immediate attack on Black's center. The idea is that it's difficult for Black to defend his e-pawn, while if he exchanges, White will be able to continue with e4-e5, chasing away Black's Knight. This variation (called the **Center Attack**) has never been wildly popular, although enterprising players try it from time to time. If Black knows what he's doing, he should be able to reach a good position.

5   ...   e5xd4

Karpov exchanges pawns rather than play d7-d6, which leaves the Knight on c6 pinned.

6   0-0

White could immediately advance with e4-e5, but he prefers to first safeguard his King.

6   ...   Bf8-e7

Black develops a piece while safeguarding his King. Taking the pawn on e4 is a too dangerous. After 6 ... Nf6xe4, White would play 7 Rf1-e1! simultaneously pinning and attacking the Knight. If Black then defends with 7 ... d7-d5, White plays 8 Nf3xd4, winning back a pawn and threatening 9 f2-f3 or 9 Nd4xc6.

7   e4-e5

Attacking the Knight and gaining some space.

7   ...   Nf6-e4

The Knight takes up a strong position in the center. Now that the e-file is closed, White will not easily be able to attack the Knight.

8   Nf3xd4

White wins back the sacrificed pawn.

8   ...   0-0

Black safeties his King and develops the Rook. As often happens in double-King-pawn openings, the early exchange of pawns in the center has simplified Black's defensive task. He should have no difficulty reaching a good position from here.

9	Nd4-f5	d7-d5!
10	Ba4xc6	b7xc6
11	Nf5xe7 check	Qd8xe7
12	Rf1-e1	

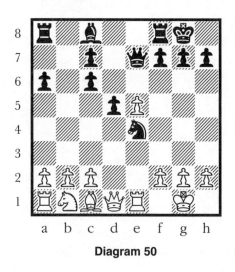

Diagram 50

Karpov has reached a very sound position, with a strong Knight on e4 backed up by pawns on d5 and c6. Although White's game appears undeveloped, there's nothing fundamentally wrong with it, as long as he can get his pieces to active squares.

12	...	Rf8-e8!

Apparently just developing the Rook, but in fact the move contains a subtle positional trap.

13	f2-f3?

White thinks this forces the Knight back to c5 and e6, after which Black will have a solid but not very menacing position. However, Karpov has a different idea.

13   ...   Ne4-d6!

The point of Black's previous move. Of course White can't play e5xd6 because of Qe7xe1 check, winning. The real point, however, is that the Knight will be able to move to f5 and later h4, creating strong attacking chances against White's King-side.

14   b2-b3

White is trying to get his pieces to useful squares. The idea of this move is to develop the Bishop to b2 or a3.

14   ...   Nd6-f5

In contrast to White, Black's pieces are moving naturally to better and better squares - the mark of a well-thought out opening plan.

15   Bc1-a3

Although this attacks the Queen, it's not particularly effective since it drives the Queen where she wants to go. White shouldn't be thinking aggressively at this point; he should be trying to equalize the game. A better try was the more modest Bc1-b2, protecting the e5-pawn one more time.

15   ...   Qe7-g4

Diagram 51

16	Ba3-b2?

White seems not to notice the danger brewing. He should have tried Qd1-d2, with the idea of exchanging Queens to break the force of Black's coming attack.

16	...	Nf5-h4

This threatens the simple and brutal Qg5xg2 mate. If White now tries to defend with Qd1-d2, Black has Nh4xf3 check!, winning the Queen because of the pin on the g-pawn. So White has to guard g2 and f3 simultaneously.

17	Qd1-e2	f7-f6!

Since the e-pawn is now pinned against the White Queen, Karpov attacks it a third time.

White is having great difficulty developing his pieces while keeping all his weak spots guarded.

18   Qe2-f2

Unpins the e-pawn.

18   ...   Bc8-h3!

Black takes advantage of another pin, this time on the g-pawn. Black now threatens the simple Bh3xg2.

19   g2-g4   f6xe5

Black pockets his first clear profit - the e-pawn. Now he threatens, among other things, h7-h5, picking off the pinned g-pawn.

Diagram 52

20   Nb1-d2?

White finally develops his Knight, but to the wrong square. Better moves were Qf2-g3 or Nb1-c3.

20	...	**Qg5xd2!**

Karpov finishes White off with a tactical shot. If White recaptures with 21 Qf2xd2, Black wins the Queen back with Nh4xf3 check and Nf3xd2. If White tries Qf2xh4, Black has Qd2-g2 mate, so White resigns.

6

BLACK "HALF-OPEN" DEFENSES

Up until now, we've only considered openings where Black responds to e2-e4 with the symmetrical ply e7-e5. Suppose Black doesn't want to respond symmetrically? Are there openings that don't start with e7-e5 for Black?

FIRST WORD

Black "half-open" defenses are becoming more popular all the time. It's not unusual, in a tournament, to see more games started with the openings in this section than with the traditional openings of our first two chapters.

The answer is: Yes, indeed. Black has a wide variety of other ways to answer e2-e4, and these "half-open games", as they're called, often lead to exciting and spirited play, where Black has both more winning chances and more losing chances than in the normal double King pawn openings.

Today's players are looking for ways to seize the initiative quickly with the Black pieces, rather than passively defending against White's attack. These openings offer that possibility. Play through our sample games and variations, and see if they don't appeal to you, too!

In this chapter we'll take a look at these openings:
- **Center Counter Defense**
- **Alekhine's Defense**
- **Caro-Kann Defense**
- **French Defense**
- **Sicilian Defense**

CENTER COUNTER DEFENSE

In the **Center Counter Defense**, Black responds to e2-e4 with the audacious thrust d7-d5:

Diagram 53

Not content to sit back passively, Black immediately rips the center open, and is prepared to violate a cherished opening principle and develop his Queen early if need be.

The Center Counter Game has never been refuted in master play, although it's certainly not to everyone's taste. It's a suitable choice for players who want an open position with active play for their pieces, but who don't want to give White the possibility of the quick attacks possible in the double King-pawn openings.

Here's a typical sequence in the **Center Counter Defense**:

	White:	Black:
1	e2-e4	d7-d5
2	e4xd5	Qd8xd5
3	Nb1-c3	

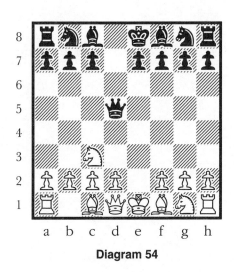

Diagram 54

White develops his Queen's Knight to its ideal square and gains time by attacking Black's Queen. Where should the Queen retreat?

3	...	Qd5-a5

Although this square looks innocuous, it's actually Black's best choice.

Black can easily get in trouble with these other moves:

a. 3 ... Qd5-c6?? loses the Queen immediately to Bf1-b5!

b. 3 ... Qd5-e5 check looks aggressive but White replies Bf1-e2, then gains more time next turn by attacking the Queen with Ng1-f3.

c. 3 ... Qd5-d8 is possible but looks abject.

4	d2-d4

White eagerly gains more ground in the center.

4	...	Ng8-f6
5	Ng1-f3	Bc8-g4

A good move. Black tries to exchange pieces to cut down White's advantages in space and time.

6	h2-h3	Bg4xf3
7	Qd1xf3	

Attacking the pawn on b7.

7	...	c7-c6

The more natural looking move, Nb8-c6, gets Black in some trouble after Bf1-b5. In these asymmetrical openings, one misstep by Black can be very costly.

8	Bf1-c4

Develops the Bishop to an active square and prepares to castle King-side.

8	...	e7-e6
9	0-0	Nb8-d7

Black's development is modest, but he's getting his pieces into play and he's avoided any disaster.

10	Bc1-f4	Bf8-e7
11	Rf1-e1	

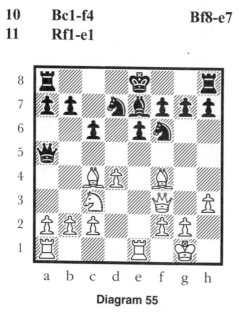

Diagram 55

White has more space, but Black's game is fundamentally solid. White will look to expand on his space advantage, perhaps with a series of moves like a2-a3, b2-b4, Bc4-b3, Nc3-a4, and c2-c4. Black will need to castle, safeguarding his King, then redeploy his Queen and try to find ways to counter White's extra space, perhaps with a plan like Qa5-c7 and c7-c5.

ALEKHINE'S DEFENSE

Alekhine's Defense is named for Alexander Alekhine, World Champion from 1927 to 1946. He introduced it into master play at the Budapest tournament in 1921. The defense is characterized by the moves:

| 1 | e2-e4 | Ng8-f6 |

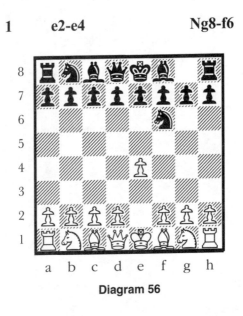

Diagram 56

The Knight's move is unlike any opening we've seen thus far: instead of moving out a central pawn to make way for the Queen and Bishops, Black instead moves out a Knight, seemingly begging White to harass it. What's going on?

The idea behind Alekhine's Defense is a clever one. Black wants White to advance his center pawns, chasing the Knight around the board. Later on, Black hopes to counterattack the center from the flanks, causing it to collapse. After the center has collapsed, Black will himself occupy the center with his own pawns and pieces, gaining the upper hand.

Alekhine's Defense is a suitable choice for counter-attacking players who don't mind giving White an early initiative, but who are adept at exploiting weaknesses left behind in an overextended position.

This radical strategy was an invention of the Hypermodern school, a collection of European masters and grandmasters that flourished in the 1920s. They invigorated chess strategy with many new ideas, of which Alekhine's Defense was just one. (We'll see other examples later in the book.)

Nowadays these ideas aren't considered particularly radical, but rather just another part of the chess player's armory.

Here's a typical line of **Alekhine's Defense**:

	White:	Black:
1	e2-e4	Ng8-f6
2	e4-e5	

Black's move says "Grab the center and see if you can keep it!". White's reply says "Thank you very much, I believe I will."

2	...	Nf6-d5
3	c2-c4	Nd5-b6
4	d2-d4	d7-d6
5	f2-f4	

Diagram 57

White has adopted the **Four Pawn's Attack**, a critical variation where White aggressively tries to refute the defense altogether. Black has to tread carefully to avoid getting squashed.

> 5   ...   d6xe5

Black needs to exchange some wood in order to get his pieces into play.

> 6   f4xe5

White doesn't recapture with the d-pawn since Black would then be able to trade Queens.

> 6   ...   Nb8-c6

The counterattack starts! Black attacks the White d-pawn with his Knight and Queen. White must start to defend his center.

	7	**Bc1-e3**

The other move, Ng1-f3, wouldn't work so well as Black would reply Bc8-g4, pinning the Knight to the Queen.

	7	...	**Bc8-f5**

Black has only moved one pawn, but already most of his pieces are in play.

8	**Nb1-c3**	**e7-e6**
9	**Ng1-f3**	**Qd8-d7**

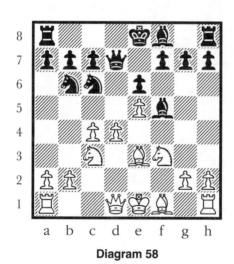

Diagram 58

Although cramped for space, Black is managing to complete his development. White's center is imposing, but *it's not threatening to go anywhere.* If White tries 10 c4-c5, Black's Knight on b6 can hop into d5. The super-aggressive 10 d4-d5 leads to wild complications after 10 ... e6xd5 11 c4xd5 Nc6-b4!

10	Bf1-e2	0-0-0

Castling Queen-side brings the Rook into play against White's d-pawn.

11	0-0	f7-f6

Black continues to snip away at the White center.

12	e5xf6	g7xf6

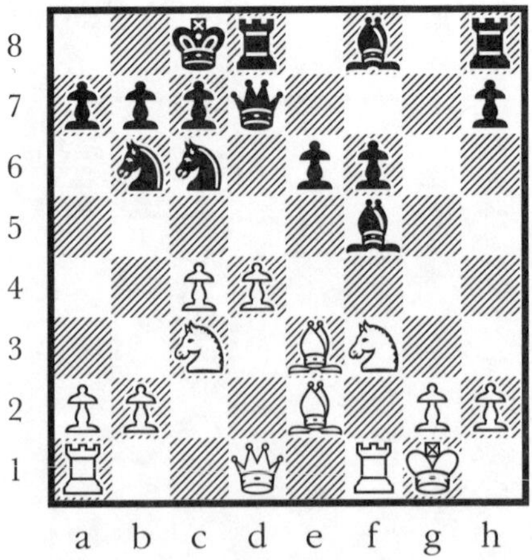

Diagram 59

A double-edged position. White still has more space, but Black's pieces are active and it will be hard for White to generate anything concrete. This unbalanced game with mutual counter-chances is the sort that modern players much prefer to play as Black. Black will play moves like Rh8-g8, Qd7-g7, and Bf8-d6 to aim for a King-side attack. White will try to use his central pawn majority to attack on the Queen-side, aiming for moves like d4-d5 or c4-c5 at the appropriate time.

CARO-KANN DEFENSE

The **Caro-Kann Defense** is characterized by:

1	e2-e4	c7-c6

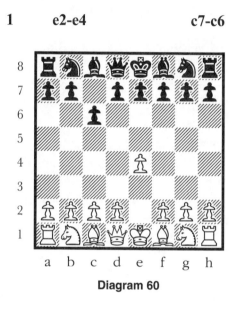

Diagram 60

The move c7-c6 looks totally innocuous but actually is part of a deeper plan. After White plays the natural d2-d4, Black will continue with d7-d5, grabbing a share of the center. Eventually Black will develop his light-squared Bishop to f5 or g4, as required, his Knights to d7 and f6, and place his e-pawn on e6.

The resulting formation will be difficult for White to overrun, although White should enjoy an advantage in space.

In practice, the **Caro-Kann** is a favorite choice of defensive-minded players who prefer a solid position to an open, tactical one. World Champions Botvinnik and Petrosian were advocates of the **Caro-Kann** in their time, and today Anatoly Karpov uses the defense frequently. Here's a typical line of the **Caro-Kann**:

	White:	Black:
1	e2-e4	c7-c6
2	d2-d4	d7-d5
3	Nb1-c3	

This move develops the Knight and defends the e-pawn. It's always been White's most popular third move, although two others have been tried from time to time: 3 e4-e5 (the **Advance Variation**) and 3 e4xd5 (the **Panov-Botvinnik Attack**).

3	...	d5xe4

It's difficult for Black to develop his game if he has to worry about the safety of the pawn on d5. Although this leaves White with a better center (a pawn on d4 versus a pawn on c6) Black hopes that easy development for his pieces will be compensation.

4	Nc3xe4	Bc8-f5

The Bishop develops and gains time by attacking the Knight.

5	Ne4-g3

The Knight retreats but turns the tables on the Bishop.

5	...	Bf5-g6
6	h2-h4	

An aggressive move designed to gain more space on the Kingside. The immediate threat is h4-h5, neatly trapping the Bishop.

6	...	h7-h6

Providing a hiding spot for the Bishop.

7	Ng1-f3	Nb8-d7

Accurate. This move prevents White from playing Nf3-e5, which would be awkward to meet.

8	h4-h5	Bg6-h7
9	Bf1-d3!	

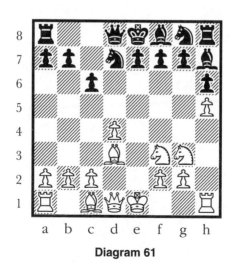

Diagram 61

107

This move forces an exchange of Bishops, which will result in a considerable lead in development for White. (He'll be exchanging a Bishop which has only moved once for a Bishop which will have moved four (!) times). However, Black's position is so compact and solid that it will be hard for White to generate much of an attack with his extra time.

9	...	Bh7xd3
10	Qd1xd3	Qd8-c7

This prevents White from developing the Bishop to the active square f4.

11	Bc1-d2

White plans on castling Queen-side, so as to leave open the possibility of advancing his pawns on the King-side, gaining space. To avoid the possibility of coming under a strong attack, Black will want to castle Queen-side as well.

11	...	e7-e6
12	0-0-0	Ng8-f6
13	Qd3-e2	0-0-0

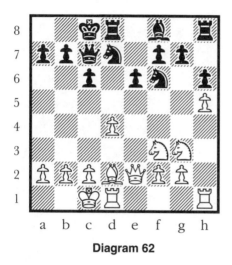

Diagram 62

White has a slight advantage in space but no major threats. Black's game is compact and solid.

White's natural plan consists of expanding in the center with c2-c4, Bd2-c3, Rh1-e1, and Nf3-e5. Black can counter this by playing Bf8-d6 and trying to exchange pieces, perhaps by moving the Bishop on to f4 or exchanging on g3.

If White overextends himself, Black may be able to infiltrate White's weak points and develop an initiative in the endgame.

FRENCH DEFENSE

The **French Defense** is a solid and unpretentious defense to e2-e4. It begins with the moves

1	e2-e4	e7-e6
2	d2-d4	d7-d5

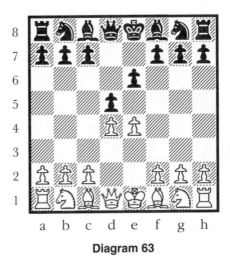

Diagram 63

Black's idea is to allow White a strong pawn center in the hopes of later attacking from the flanks with moves like c7-c5 and f7-f6. Usually, White tries to use his advantage in space to build up a winning attack in the middle game. If that attack runs out of steam, however, Black often gains the upper hand in the endgame.

The French Defense is an excellent defense for players who want a game with a locked pawn structure and a minimum of early tactics, combined with the possibility of strong counterattacking chances later in the game.

In the French Defense, the center pawns often become blocked, with White's pawns usually at e4 and e5, and Black's pawns at e6 and d5. White naturally attacks on the King-side, where he has more space, while Black usually counters on the Queen-side. The French Defense avoids the wide-open piece play and speculative attacks associated with the double King-pawn openings, and is a good way to defuse the attacking possibilities many players expect to obtain with the White pieces.

The French Defense dates back to the early nineteenth century, when it was used by the French players in a correspondence match between Paris and London. It's never really gone out of fashion, although it's not as popular as it once was.

Here's a fairly typical variation of the French:

	White:	Black:
1	e2-e4	e7-e6
2	d2-d4	d7-d5
3	Nb1-c3	

Defends the e-pawn. If Black captures, White can re-capture and have a strong Knight in the center of the board.

3	...	Ng8-f6

Renews the attack against the e-pawn. Black is trying to force White to either advance the pawn or exchange it. Either way, the tension in the center will be resolved, after which Black can plan his strategy more clearly.

4	Bc1-g5	

White defends his pawn by pinning the attacking Knight.

4	...	Bf8-e7

111

Black unpins the Knight, thus renewing the attack on the pawn.

5   e4-e5

White finally releases the tension, but gains ground in the process.

5   ...   Nf6-d7
6   Bg5xe7   Qd8xe7

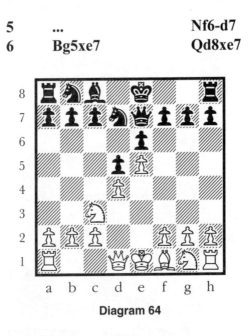

Diagram 64

Both players gained something from the last exchange. By exchanging a piece, Black relieved the cramp in his game to some extent. White is happy because he exchanged a *bad Bishop* for a *good Bishop*.

A **bad Bishop** is a Bishop that is blocked by its own center pawns. Since White's center pawns are now permanently fixed on dark squares, his dark-squared Bishop is "bad." A **good Bishop** is a Bishop that travels on the opposite-colored squares from his center pawns.

Black's center pawns are now fixed on light squares, so his dark-squared Bishop is "good" and his light-squared Bishop is "bad." Bad Bishops are less useful since they have less to attack, so you should be glad to exchange a "bad" one for a "good" one.

7	Qd1-d2

White clears the back rank and prepares to castle Queen-side. This will free his King-side pawns to advance, gaining more space.

7	...	0-0
8	f2-f4	

Supports the center and gains more space. White doesn't mind placing all his pawns on dark squares since his dark-squared Bishop is gone and can't be impeded.

8	...	c7-c5

Black begins his counter-attack against the White center. Advancing the c-pawn both attacks the d-pawn and gains some space on the Queen-side.

Games in which the players attack on opposite sides of the board tend to be especially exciting and double-edged. Victory goes to the player whose attack can crash through first.

9	Ng1-f3	Nb8-c6
10	d4xc5!	

113

Diagram 65

A good play. White wants to keep as many pieces on the board as possible, so he exchanges pawns first. If he had waited, Black would himself have captured on d4, forcing an exchange of Knights. The fewer pieces on the board, the easier it will be for Black to equalize.

| 10 | ... | Nd7xc5 |
| 11 | 0-0-0 | a7-a6 |

The pawn move prepares b7-b5 followed by a general advance against White's King.

| 12 | Bf1-d3! | |

This move is part of a regrouping strategy to bring White's pieces to their best positions. White knows that his Knight on c3 will eventually be driven away from its post when Black plays b7-b5-b4, so he prepares to redeploy it by the maneuver Nc3-e2-d4, bringing it to a square (d4) where it can't be attacked by enemy pawns. But first White develops the Bishop to a useful square. If Black captures the Bishop by Nc5xd3 check, White plans to recapture by c2xd3! after which he will bring his Knight to d4, his King to b1, and his Rook to c1. This far-sighted plan should give White a slight edge in the middlegame.

| 12 | ... | b7-b5 |

Black continues with his advance on the Queen-side. He has nothing better.

13	Nc3-e2	Bc8-b7
14	Ne2-d4	Nc6xd4
15	Nf3xd4	Ra8-c8

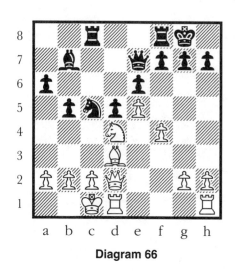

Diagram 66

White has a slight advantage because of the strong position of his Knight in the center and the greater activity of his "good" Bishop compared to Black's "bad" Bishop. From this position, White can try to mount a King-side attack with moves like Rh1-e1-e3-h3, or h2-h4-h5 followed by Rh1-h3-g3. Black can expand on the Queenside by playing Rc8-c7 and Rf8-c8, or counterattack the White center with f7-f6 at the proper time.

SICILIAN DEFENSE

The **Sicilian Defense** has been one of the most popular openings for the last fifty years or so. The reason is simple: it leads to complex, unbalanced positions, where Black has a fighting chance to seize the initiative early in the game.

In most other defenses, Black must first survive White's attack, and only then press for an advantage. The play in the **Sicilian Defense** is so complicated that Black may find himself in a winning position after just a few moves! The **Sicilian Defense** begins with these moves:

1   e2-e4   c7-c5

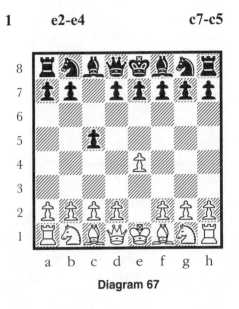

Diagram 67

By advancing his c-pawn, Black announces his intentions from the beginning: he is carving out space on the Queen-side, while allowing White the upper hand on the King-side. As the game develops, each side presses its attack in the area where they have the most space - White on the King-side, Black on the Queen-side.

To make the game even more exciting, the players often castle on opposite sides of the board, so each player's attack ends up directed at the enemy King. The result is double-edged, exciting chess, with victory or defeat often balanced on a razor's edge.

The Sicilian Defense is an excellent choice for Black players who want to play for a win with an uncompromising fight from the first move.

We'll look at three games to give you a flavor of **Sicilian Defense** play. The first is from 1942 in Budapest, a game in which a couple of early errors by Black lead to a quick kill.

KLUGER VS. NAGY

White (Kluger)		Black (Nagy)
1	e2-e4	c7-c5
2	Ng1-f3	Nb8-c6
3	d2-d4	

Standard play in the **Sicilian Defense**. White advances his d-pawn, opening up more space for his Queen and Queen's Bishop.

3	...	c5xd4

| 4 | Nf3xd4 | Ng8-f6 |

Attacking White's e-pawn.

| 5 | Nb1-c3 | d7-d6 |

Black has a number of ways to arrange his pieces and pawns for the upcoming struggle. The method chosen in this game, involving moving the Knights to c6 and f6 and the d-pawn to d6, is one of the most common.

| 6 | Bc1-g5 | a7-a6 |

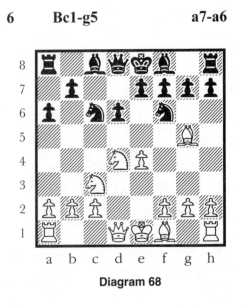

Diagram 68

This, however, is an error. Black would do better to play e7-e6 followed by Bf8-e7, developing the King-side pieces and preparing to castle. In sharp openings like the Sicilian, inaccuracies are often quickly punished.

| 7 | Qd1-d2 | Nf6-d7? |

Another inaccuracy. Black should be developing more pieces, rather than shifting around his Knights. Once again, e7-e6 was better.

8   Bf1-e2   g7-g6

Black wants to develop his Bishop to g7, followed by King-side castling. But he's ceded a lot of time and space to White, and problems start brewing immediately.

9   Nc3-d5!

White takes charge. Black is in a lot of trouble.

9   ...   f7-f6

Trying to drive away the Bishop so as to continue with Bf8-g7. Black has seen that immediately playing 9 ... Nf8-g7 is answered by 10 Nd4xc6! b7xc6 11 Bg5xe7. However, his actual move has an even more attractive refutation.

10   Nd4-e6!

The Knight exploits the undefended square at e6.

10   ...   Qd8-a5

The only safe square for the Queen.

11   Nd5-c7 check   Ke8-f7

The only square for the King.

12	Ne6-d8 check!	Kf7-g7

If Black captures the Knight by Nc6xd8, White has Qd2xa5!

13	Nc7-e8 check!	Resigns

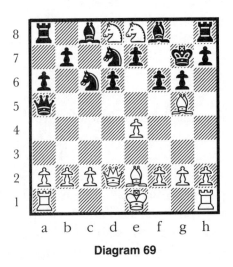

Diagram 69

An amusing position. On move 13 White's two Knights have penetrated to d8 and e8! Black gives up because of 13 ... Kg7-g8 (forced) 14 Be2-c4 check! will eventually force checkmate after Black sacrifices his d-pawn and e-pawn.

The next game, from 1976, shows Black beating off an apparently vicious attack, then controlling the board with his pieces.

BONO VS. ROBERTIE

	White (Bono)	Black (Robertie)
1	e2-e4	c7-c5
2	Ng1-f3	d7-d6
3	d2-d4	c5xd4
4	Nf3xd4	Ng8-f6
5	Nb1-c3	a7-a6

Black has played a slightly different move order from the previous game. This is called the **Najdorf Variation**, a favorite of both Bobby Fischer and Gary Kasparov, and one of the most complicated variations in chess.

| 6 | Bc1-g5 | e7-e6 |

In contrast to the previous game, Black prepares to develop his King's Bishop to e7.

| 7 | f2-f4 | |

The move grabs more space on the King-side and controls the e5 square.

| 7 | ... | Bf8-e7 |

Develops the Bishop and breaks the pin on the Knight.

| 8 | Qd1-f3 | h7-h6 |

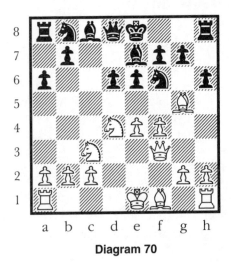

Diagram 70

This innocuous-looking attack on the Bishop is actually the start of an audacious plan to break the back of White's King-side pressure. The game will soon become tremendously complicated.

9   Bg5-h4

White doesn't want to exchange by 9 Bg5xf6 Be7xf6. In these open positions, long-ranging Bishops are usually stronger than Knights.

9   ...   g7-g5!

The point of this move is to dislodge White's f-pawn, so that Black can maneuver a Knight to the e5-square, where it will dominate the center.

10   f4xg5   Nf6-d7

Notice that White's pawn on g5 is now pinned against the Bishop on h4. Meanwhile, the pawn is attacked three times (by the Queen, Bishop, and pawn on h6), and defended only once. And the Black Knight is ready to hop into the strong square e5. Black's plan seems to be working, but White has a shot.

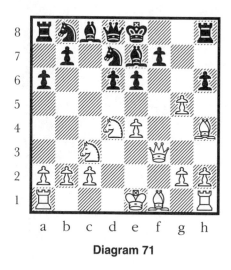

Diagram 71

11   Nd4xe6!

White sacrifices a Knight to open up attacking lines against Black's King.

11   ...   f7xe6
12   Qf3-h5 check

This check prevents Black from castling, and drives the Black King onto the open f-file, where White's Rooks can get at him.

12	...	Ke8-f8
13	Bf1-b5!	

Since any move of the Bishop threatens 14 0-0 check and
15 Qh5-f7 mate, White knows Black won't have time to
capture the Bishop wherever he puts it, so he picks the
most aggressive square.

| 13 | ... | Rh8-h7! |

White is threatening an eventual checkmate on the f7
square, so Black moves his Rook to the defense of that
square. In subsequent play, the Rook will form a shield
in front of the Black King, even while all his pawns are
stripped away.

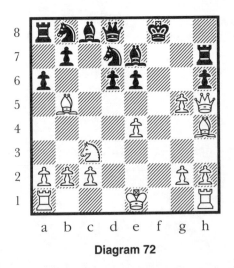

Diagram 72

| 14 | Qh5-g6 |

Attacks the undefended Rook and guards the g8 square,
renewing the threat of 15 0-0 check. (Castling immedi-

ately would be answered by Kf8-g8.)

14	...	Rh7-f7!

Black's game just barely hangs together. The Rook takes over the f-file, preventing White from castling. Black's King will be stripped of his pawn cover, however.

15	Qg6xh6 check	

The h-pawn goes.

15	...	Kf8-g8
16	Qh6-g6 check	Rf7-g7

The Rook shields the King, but now the e-pawn goes.

17	Qg6-e6 check	Kg8-h8

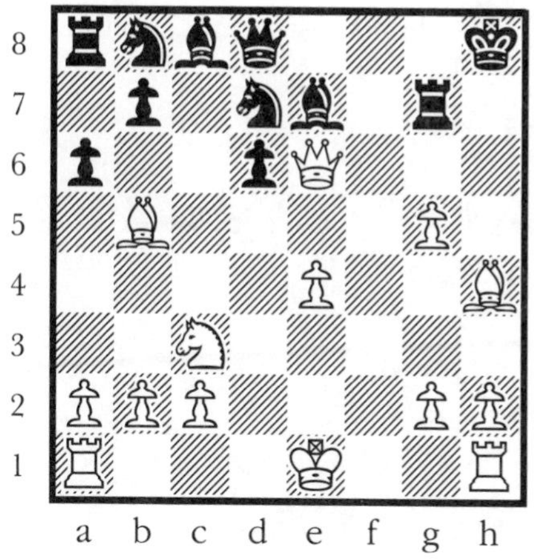

Diagram 73

Let's take a look. White is now ahead in material. His
rampaging Queen has managed to snare four pawns for
the sacrificed Knight. However, the worst is now over
for Black. His King has reached comparative safety at h8
(Qe6-h6 check is answered by Rg7-h7, and White is out
of checks) and now Black's pieces can start to occupy
some of the available squares in the center.

This is always the great danger for White in the Sicilian
- if his initial attack runs out of gas, the initiative may
revert to Black.

18   Bb5xd7

Black was now threatening to capture the Bishop at
long last.

18   ...   Nb8-d7

The Knight is headed for the great square at e5.

19   0-0   Nd7-e5

Occupies the e5 square, and uncovers an attack on the
Queen by the Bishop.

20   Qe6-d5

If 20 Qe6-h6 check, Black replies with Rg7-h7 and the
Queen is trapped!

20   ...   Bc8-g4
21   Bh4-g3

White feels the Knight is too powerful on e5, and wants to exchange it for the relatively inactive Bishop.

| 21 | ... | Rg7xg5 |

Black wins back a pawn and prepares to recapture on e5 with the Rook.

| 22 | Bg3xe5 | Rg5xe5 |
| 23 | Qd5-d4 | |

Pins the Rook to the Black King.

| 23 | ... | Be7-f6 |

Unpins the Rook and activates the Bishop.

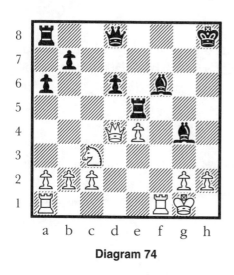

Diagram 74

| 24 | Nc3-d5 |

White's Knight grabs an excellent square in the center of the board.

| 24 | ... | Bf6-g7 |

White was threatening to capture the Bishop, so Black moves it to safety. From g7, the bishop guards the King and indirectly threatens the White Queen. Notice that although Black's King has been stripped of his pawn protection, Black's pieces have taken up the job of guarding all the approaches to the King.

| 25 | Rf1-f7 |

Attacks the b-pawn and grabs the seventh rank.

| 25 | ... | Qd8-g5! |

Black lets the b-pawn go and switches over to the attack. If White tries 26 Rf7xb7, Black will play the powerful 26 ... Bg4-f3!, threatening Qg5xg2 mate and Bf3xe4.

| 26 | Nd5-c3 |

The Knight retreats to add extra protection to the e-pawn.

| 26 | ... | Re5-e7! |

Double attack! The Bishop attacks the Queen, while Black's Rook attacks White's Rook. Only one move saves both pieces.

27	Qd4-f2

The Queen moves away and defends the Rook.

27	...	Re7xf7
28	Qf2xf7	Ra8-f8

Another attack on the Queen. More important, notice how all Black's pieces are being brought to bear on White's King.

29	Qf7-d5

Hoping to ward off the attack by exchanging Queens.

29	...	Bg7-e5!

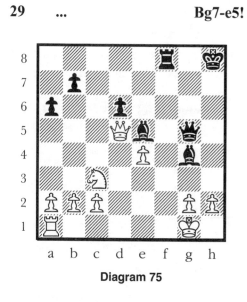

Diagram 75

Black will have none of that! He uses the Bishop to block the attack on the Queen. At the same time, the Bishop takes aim at the h2 square.

Notice how important the square e5 has been for Black. He has occupied it successively with his Knight, his Rook, and finally his Bishop. Each piece has added its weight to the growing pressure on White's position.

| 30 | Qd5-d3 | Qg5-f4! |

Threatens 31 ... Qf4xh2 mate, an unstoppable threat.

| 31 | g2-g3 | Qf4-f2 check |
| 32 | Resigns | |

White is forced to play Kg1-h1, after which Bg4-f3 check wins the Queen. White gives up.

GELLER VS. VATNIKOV

Our third and last **Sicilian** game features the Soviet players Geller and Vatnikov. It was played in 1950.

	White (Geller)	Black (Vatnikov)
1	e2-e4	c7-c5
2	Ng1-f3	Nb8-c6
3	d2-d4	c5xd4
4	Nf3xd4	Ng8-f6
5	Nb1-c3	d7-d6

So far, the same moves as in our first game. Now White tries a different approach.

| 6 | Bf1-c4 | |

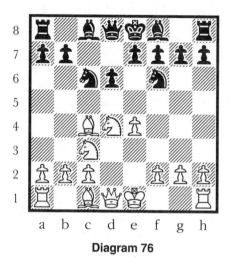

Diagram 76

White develops his King's Bishop to an active diagonal, where it strikes at the f7 square. In later years, this move became a favorite of Bobby Fischer's.

6	...	e7-e6

Although this shuts in the light-squared Bishop, it prepares to develop the dark-squared Bishop and additionally closes off the White Bishop's diagonal.

7	0-0	Bf8-e7
8	Bc1-e3	0-0
9	Bc4-b3	

While this retreat looks defensive, experience shows that the Bishop will eventually be forced to retreat here anyway, so White makes the play now while waiting to decide how to deploy the rest of his pieces.

9	...	Nc6-a5

Black prepares to trade off the relatively active White Bishop for his own relatively inactive Knight.

10   f2-f4

White starts gaining space on the Kingside.

10   ...   b7-b6

This move, preparing to develop the Bishop at b7 attacking the e-pawn, was a favorite of former World Champion Botvinnik. Another plan is 10 ... Na5xb3 11 a2xb3 d6-d5, which leads to a more simplified position.

11   e4-e5!

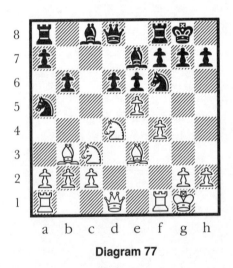

Diagram 77

White attacks immediately in the center.

11   ...   Nf6-e8

Black retreats the Knight. He could exchange pawns first and then retreat the Knight, but exchanging opens the f-file for White's Rook at f1 and the diagonal e3-h6 for White's Bishop at e3. Black reasons that he's better off leaving those lines closed.

12   f4-f5!

White, of course, tries to open those very same lines. The move he plays involves the sacrifice of the pawn at e5. White, however, has calculated the consequences.

12   ...   d6xe5

Black will be subjected to a fierce attack in any event, so he grabs a pawn and awaits developments.

13   f5xe6!

White plunges ahead. The apparent sacrifice of the Knight on d4 is only an illusion. If Black captures with 13 ... e5xd4, White regains his piece with 14 e6xf7 check Kg8-h8 15 f7xe8(Q), with the better game.

13   ...   f7-f6

Black attempts to shore up his game by building an unbridgeable wall of pawns. Unfortunately, White's Knights prove more than adequate for breaching the barricades.

14   Nd4-f5   Na5xb3

Black can't exchange Queens without losing a piece: if

14 ... Qd8xd1 15 Nf5xe7 check Kg8-f8 16 Ra1xd1.

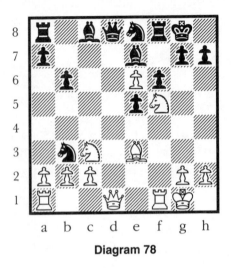

Diagram 78

15   Nc3-d5!

White doesn't waste time capturing the Knight on b3 but instead blasts his way home. This isn't really a sacrifice since White threatens to regain the piece in two different ways: either by a2xb3, or by Nd5xe7 check followed by Qd1xd8. Black is busted.

15   ...   Nb3-d4

Black moves the Knight to block the d-file. However, White wins Black's Queen from another direction.

16	Nd5xe7 check	Kg8-h8
17	Ne7-g6 check	Resigns

Black gives up in light of 17 ... h7xg6 18 e6-e7! Q moves 19 e7xf8(Q) check.

7

THE QUEEN'S GAMBIT

Up to now, we've only considered openings where White begins by moving his King's pawn with e2-e4. Those are the most important openings for players to learn.

You'll find that when you play Black, most of your opponents will open the game with e2-e4, so it's important for you to learn

FIRST WORD

In this chapter, we'll look at variations of the Queen's Gambit, the main opening in which Black responds to White's d2-d4 with d7-d5. In the final chapter, we'll look at openings where Black answers with other moves.

quickly one or two defenses against those openings.

I recommend that you open with e2-e4 when you have the chance. The openings that begin with e2-e4 tend to lead to sharp, tactical positions, whereas those that begin with d2-d4 tend to lead to slower, more closed positions in which strategical judgement plays a larger role.

When you're learning the game, you need to learn tactics and attack before you learn about strategy and defense. Tactics are simply more fundamental to your eventual success and progress. So - start playing the King's pawn openings!

Having said that, it's also true that not all your opponents will oblige by playing e2-e4 against you, so you'll need to know something about the Queen's pawn openings. And you may want to try some of these openings yourself, for variety's sake.

The **Queen's Gambit** is marked by these moves:

1	d2-d4	d7-d5
2	c2-c4	

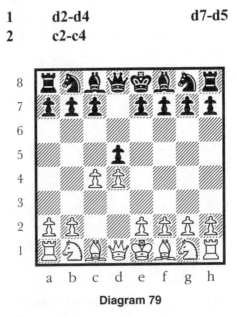

Diagram 79

White offers his c-pawn as a gambit. If Black captures, White hopes to control the center later with e2-e4.

Note that this isn't really much of a gambit. If Black captures with d5xc4, White can immediately regain the pawn, if he wishes, by Qd1-a4 check and Qa4xc4. White has other ways to eventually regain the pawn, so he rarely resorts to immediate recapture.

Black has three main defenses to the Queen's Gambit:

1. Accepting the gambit, with 2 ... d5xc4.

2. Declining the gambit and bolstering the pawn center with 2 ... e7-e6.

3. Declining the gambit and reinforcing with c7-c6.

Line 1 is called the **Queen's Gambit Accepted**. It has the virtue for Black of avoiding the cramped positions that can result in the other two lines, but White can sometimes build up a strong attack. Line 2 often leads to what is called the **Orthodox Defense**, it's a safe, solid way of continuing, although not particularly exciting or dynamic. Line 3 leads to the **Slav Defense**. It's a riskier variation, with more opportunities for counter-punching.

THE QUEEN'S GAMBIT ACCEPTED

The **Queen's Gambit Accepted** starts with these moves:

1	d2-d4	d7-d5
2	c2-c4	d5xc4

Black wastes no time and immediately grabs the gambit pawn. This saves Black from worrying about how to defend his center later on, but at the cost of giving White a relatively free hand in the center.

Unlike the case with the **King's Gambit**, Black has no real possibilities of holding onto the gambit pawn. In fact, if White chooses he can regain the pawn immediately by Qd1-a4 check and Qa4xc4. Usually, however, White postpones regaining the pawn for a few moves while he proceeds with rapid development.

Here's a typical start for the **Queen's Gambit Accepted**:

3	Ng1-f3	Ng8-f6
4	e2-e3	e7-e6
5	Bf1xc4	Bf8-e7
6	0-0	c7-c5

For a complete example of the **Queen's Gambit Accepted** and some more discussion of the underlying strategy, see *Beginning Chess Play* in this series.

THE ORTHODOX DEFENSE

The **Orthodox Defense**, marked by defending the d-pawn with 2... e7-e6, has been a solid way of handling the defense for almost a century. Black's idea is to hold onto the pawn at d5 at all cost, preventing White from playing e2-e4. Although the pawn at e6 blocks the White-squared Bishop from developing, Black hopes to bring this piece into play at a later stage.

The Orthodox Defense offers a super-solid road to equality, but it's difficult for Black to do much more unless White makes some errors.

1	d2-d4	d7-d5
2	c2-c4	e7-e6
3	Nb1-c3	Ng8-f6

Both sides develop their Knights. White's move puts additional pressure on d5; Black's move neutralizes this pressure.

4   Bc1-g5

Diagram 80

As in the Ruy Lopez, White develops his Bishop and attacks the defending Knight. Here the move contains a threat which Black must counter. White intends to play 5 c4xd5 e6xd5 6 Bg5xf6! If Black retakes with his Queen, the pawn at d5 will be lost, while if Black recaptures with his pawn at g7 his King-side pawn structure will be shattered.

4   ...   Bf8-e7

Black parries the threat while developing his Bishop, unpinning his Knight, and preparing to castle. A good multi-purpose move.

139

5	e2-e3

Having developed one Bishop, White now opens a line to develop the other. Also, the Bishop takes up the job of defending the gambit pawn on c4.

5	...	0-0

While awaiting developments, Black safeguards his King and mobilizes the Rook.

6	Ng1-f3

The Knight develops to its most natural square. White didn't want to move his Bishop on f1 yet for two good reasons:

1. It's not clear where the Bishop wants to be, on d3 or e2. On the other hand, it's clear the Knight wants to be on f3 where it attacks the vital center squares d4 and e5.

2. If Black captures on c4, White recaptures with the Bishop. If White develops the Bishop this turn, Black captures on c4 and White moves the Bishop again to recapture. This represents what we call in chess a *loss of tempo:* White will have moved the Bishop twice to reach a square that it could have reached in one move. Lost tempos represent lost time, and good players avoid that when possible.

6	...	Nb8-d7

Black, on the other hand, doesn't develop his Knight to the "natural" square c6. The reason is somewhat subtle.

Experience has shown that for Black to get an equal game in the Queen's Gambit, his c-pawn must eventually be able to move to either c6 (to support the d5-pawn) or c5 (to challenge White's d4-pawn). Black needs to develop his Knight but keep open the later possibility of c7-c6 or c7-c5. Hence the conservative move to d7.

Diagram 81

7	Ra1-c1

As before, White delays moving his white-squared Bishop, in the hope that Black will capture on c4 and White will be able to move the Bishop and recapture in one fell swoop. Instead, he develops the Rook to the useful c1 square, looking ahead to the moment when the c-file will be opened and the Rook will become active.

7	...	c7-c6

Black adds support to the pawn on d5. This extra support may, later, enable Black to plan the center break e6-e5.

8   **Bf1-d3**

White decides that he can't delay any longer in developing the Bishop, even though this will cost him a tempo. White has run out of other constructive developing moves.

8   ...   **d5xc4**

Black surrenders his center pawn but gains a tempo by forcing the Bishop to move a second time. Black will need to find some way to play either c7-c5 or e6-e5 at some point in the near future; otherwise, White's center pawn at d4 combined with his extra space will give him a permanent advantage.

9   **Bd3xc4**

White naturally recaptures.

Diagram 82

9	...	Nf6-d5

This is a characteristic freeing move for Black when defending against the Queen's Gambit. The purpose of the move is to initiate a series of exchanges. Black threatens to exchange the dark-squared Bishops, as well as the Knight on d5 for the Knight on c3. Since Black's position is more cramped than White's, some exchanges will make his position less congested and hence more defensible.

This is a good general principle to remember when defending any cramped position: *Try to exchange pieces.*

10	Bg5xe7

White has little choice. The only move which prevents exchange of the dark-squared Bishops, Bg5-f4, permits Black to play Nd5xf4, permanently damaging White's pawn structure by doubling his pawns.

10	...	Qd8xe7

The Queen recaptures, moves off the first rank, and adds some support to the squares e5 and c5, which Black hopes to use for a counterattack against the White center.

11	0-0

Capturing with 11 Nc3xd5 would be a big mistake. Black would recapture with e6xd5, re-establishing equality in the center, and moves Nd7-f6-e4, placing a powerful Knight on the e4 square. Black's game would then be at least as good as White's.

11   ...   Nd5xc3

Black continues his plan of exchanging pieces to lessen the congestion in his position.

12   Rc1xc3

White naturally recaptures with the Rook, both for pressure along the c-file, and with the possibility of eventually maneuvering along the third rank.

Diagram 83

12   ...   e6-e5

Black advances his e-pawn, a characteristic freeing maneuver in this defense. If White now exchanges, Black will recapture with his Knight, and the resulting trade of Knights will continue to free Black's cramped position. If White doesn't exchange, Black will either play e5xd4, exchanging pawns in the center, or e5-e4, grabbing some more center territory.

13	d4xe5

White elects to exchange, hoping after the trades to launch an attack on the King-side.

13	...	Nd7xe5

Black's recapture is forced.

14	Nf3xe5	Qe7xe5

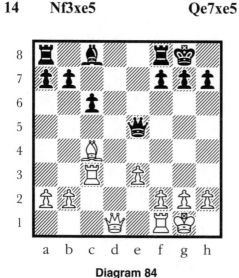

Diagram 84

The exchanges leave White with two small assets: a better development of his pieces (compare White's Bishop and Rook with Black's) and a majority of pawns on the King-side, where White has four pawns to Black's three. Can White exploit these advantages? The judgment of master opinion is that Black can work his way to equality with accurate play.

15	f2-f4!

This is the best chance for an advantage. White hopes to push his pawn to f5, where it will both cramp Black's Bishop and increase the scope of White's Rooks.

| 15 | ... | Qe5-e4 |

The Queen blocks the advance of White's e-pawn.

| 16 | Bc4-b3 |

White would like to chase the Black Queen away with Bc4-d3, but that allows Black to capture the e-pawn. Instead, White maneuvers the Bishop to c2 via b3.

| 16 | ... | Bc8-f5 |

Black's pieces are out and he has solved most of his opening problems. White will try to chase Black's Queen from the powerful post at e4 with an eventual Bb3-c2, followed by exchanging Bishops. If White can play e3-e4 at some point, he may gain an advantage. Black will try to occupy the central files with his Rooks and keep White's pawn at e3. If he can do that, he should have no problems. The game is about even.

SLAV DEFENSE
In the **Slav Defense**, Black defends his d-pawn by c7-c6 instead of e7-e6, thereby keeping a diagonal open for his Queen's Bishop. Black's game is typically less cramped than in the Orthodox Defense, with more opportunity for active play.

At the same time, White also has extra attacking chances, so the play is frequently lively and dynamic.

Overall, the Slav Defense is a good choice for players who want some real counter-attacking chances as Black, without incurring the risk of the Indian defenses (next chapter).

| 1 | d2-d4 | d7-d5 |
| 2 | c2-c4 | c7-c6 |

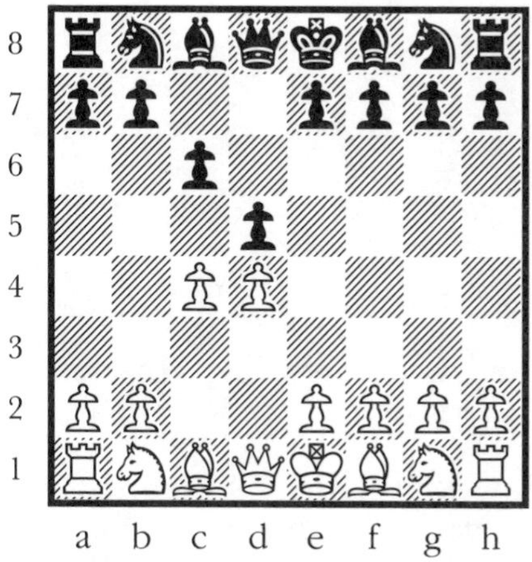

Diagram 85

The characteristic move of the Slav Defense. Black guards the d-pawn while keeping a diagonal open for the Bishop to develop to f5.

| 3 | Ng1-f3 | Ng8-f6 |
| 4 | Nb1-c3 | d5xc4 |

Both sides develop their Knights to the natural squares. Black's capture is not really an attempt to win a pawn, since White can easily force the recapture of the pawn. Rather, Black is hoping that the time it takes White to recapture will enable Black to complete the development of his pieces.

5	a2-a4

Time-wasting but necessary. White couldn't permit Black to play b7-b5, which would guard the pawn on c4 and ensure that Black remained a pawn ahead.

5	...	Bc8-f5

Black develops his Bishop and prevents White from playing e2-e4.

6	e2-e3

White opens up a line for his King's Bishop and prepares to recapture on c4.

6	...	e7-e6
7	Bf1xc4	Bf8-b4

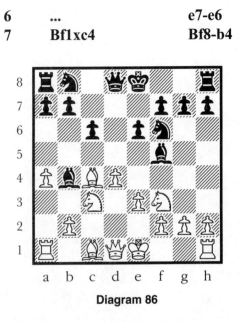

Diagram 86

White has recaptured the pawn. However, Black has achieved very active play for his pieces. The Bishop at b4 pins the Knight to White's King.

8   0-0   0-0

Both sides take time to safeguard their Kings.

9   Qd1-e2

White places the Queen behind the e-pawn and now threatens to take over the center with e3-e4! Black must find a defense.

9   ...   Bf5-g4

Black defends against the advance of the e-pawn with a counterattack against the White Knight. If White now tries to play e3-e4, Black will respond with Bg4xf3, knocking out the last support of the d-pawn, followed by Qd8xd4.

10   Rf1-d1

White guards the d-pawn, thus renewing the threat of e3-e4.

10   ...   Nb8-d7

Black decides that he can no longer prevent the advance of the pawn to e4. Instead, he finishes his development, relying on active piece play to combat White's center predominance.

11   e2-e4

White finally establishes two pawns abreast in the center.

11   ...   Qd8-e7

And Black completes his development.

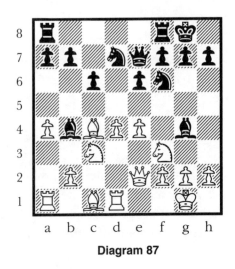

Diagram 87

12   h2-h3

White attacks the Bishop, to eliminate the annoying pin that ties down his Queen.

12   ...   Bg4xf3

Retreating the Bishop allows White to gain space on the King-side with g2-g4 and Nf3-h4. Black instead decides to exchange and counter-attack in the center.

13   Qe2xf3   e6-e5!

This characteristic thrust breaks up White's pawn center.

14	d4-d5

Although White wasn't able to maintain two pawns abreast in the center, he emerges with a slight advantage in space after this move.

14	...	Nd7-b6
15	Bc4-b3	

White has more space and greater freedom for his pieces. Slight advantage to White. White should strive to gain more space with moves like a4-a5, Bc1-g5, and Ra1-c1. Black will have to counter with defensive moves like a7-a5, h7-h6, and the development of the Rooks to c8 and d8.

8

THE INDIAN DEFENSES

The term **Indian Defenses** loosely refer to those opening where Black responds to White's d2-d4 with a move other than d7-d5.

We'll consider these three main defenses in this chapter:

FIRST WORD

The term **Indian Defenses** loosely refer to those opening where Black responds to White's d2-d4 with a move other than d7-d5.

Let's check them out!

- **Nimzo-Indian Defense**
- **Gruenfeld Defense**
- **King's Indian Defense**

Legend has it that these openings were first played in the West by British soldiers returning from India in the late nineteenth century, where they had learned the formations from native Indians, who were playing a slightly modified form of chess. The openings didn't catch on until the mid-twentieth century, when they became, as a group, the most important defenses to d2-d4.

The Indian Defenses are based upon counter-attack. In the **Nimzo-Indian**, White is prevented from playing e2-

e4 by pressure against his center from Black's pieces. In the **Gruenfeld** and **King's Indian**, Black actually allows White to build up an imposing center, then attempts to chip it away from the flanks.

All three openings lead to sharp, double-edged positions where Black has chances not just to equalize, but to actually seize the advantage. Small wonder that they have become Black's weapon of choice in meeting the Queen's Pawn openings.

NIMZO-INDIAN DEFENSE

The **Nimzo-Indian Defense** (named after the Danish grandmaster Aron Nimzovich) is characterized by these three moves:

1	d2-d4	Ng8-f6
2	c2-c4	e7-e6
3	Nb1-c3	Bf8-b4

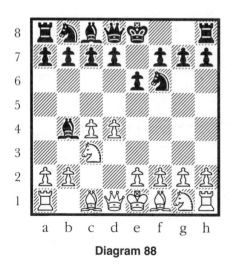

Diagram 88

With Black's first move, Ng8-f6, he prevents White from occupying the center by attacking the e4 square with a piece rather than a pawn. White's third move, Nb1-c3, again threatens to push e2-e4, and Black's third move, Bishop to b4, stops this thrust by pinning the Knight against the King.

This theme of restraint continues throughout the opening. White tries to enforce e2-e4; Black looks for ways to prevent it. Black may eventually play d7-d5, but at a time and place of his own choosing. Black's position is usually flexible and dynamic, and it's hard for White to achieve more than a slight initiative.

The **Nimzo-Indian Defense** offers Black more dynamic play than most lines of the Queen's Gambit. It's a good defense for players who want an unbalanced position, without conceding too much central play to White. Here's a sample opening line:

1	d2-d4	Ng8-f6
2	c2-c4	e7-e6
3	Nb1-c3	Bf8-b4
4	e2-e3	

White can try many different moves here. Besides e2-e3, which has always been considered the main line, White can also play Qd1-c2, Qd1-b3, Ng1-f3, Bc1-g5, a2-a3, f2-f3, and g2-g3. All lead to interesting play, and none is considered a refutation of the Nimzo-Indian.

The idea of e2-e3 is simply to proceed with development. White plans to play Ng1-f3, Bf1-d3, and 0-0. His later plan will depend on exactly how Black arranges his pieces. White will postpone any attempt at e3-e4 until much later in the game.

| 4 | ... | 0-0 |

This is Black's most flexible move. He's not yet sure where he wants to put his center pawns, so he postpones that decision and instead makes a move that he knows he'll make at some point anyway. This is sound strategy in many opening situations: *Make the least committal move first, and save the more committal moves for later, when the position has begun to take shape.*

| 5 | Bf1-d3 |

A good developing move which, incidentally, threatens to play e3-e4. Black will prevent this.

| 5 | ... | d7-d5 |

Nails down the e4 square and grabs some more room in the center.

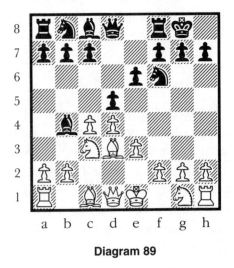

Diagram 89

6	Ng1-f3	c7-c5

Black continues to fight for space and attacks White's center.

7	0-0

Safeguards the King and unpins the Knight on c3.

7	...	Nb8-c6

Compare this position to Black's position after seven moves in the Orthodox Defense to the Queen's Gambit. Black has more space and a much freer position, while White's game is less imposing.

8	a2-a3

Black's extra freedom has been purchased at a small price, however. This move forces Black to exchange Bishop for Knight, leaving White with a small advantage. A position with two Bishops is thought to offer more promise, because of the Bishop's extra mobility, to one with two Knights.

8 ... Bb4xc3

If Black retreats the Bishop (to a5), he gives up protection of the pawn on c5. White would then play d4xc5, winning a pawn, at least temporarily.

9 b2xc3

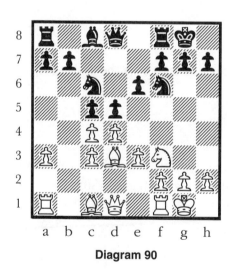

Diagram 90

9 ... d5xc4

This is one way to handle the position, although it's by no means forced. Black could also try Qd8-c7 or b7-b6, with the idea of developing the Bishop to b7. The idea behind the exchange is to move White's Bishop to an unguarded square. Later on, Black may gain a tempo by attacking the Bishop.

10   Bd3xc4   Qd8-c7

The Queen lines up on the c-file opposite White's now-unguarded Bishop. From c7, the Queen also supports the freeing maneuver e6-e5.

11   Rf1-e1

White continues to play for e3-e4. However, Black gets there first.

11   ...   e6-e5!

If Black gets this move in, he is usually guaranteed equal play.

12   d4-d5

A sharp move which aims at getting the pawn to d6, where it will threaten the Queen and cramp Black's game.

12   ...   Nc6-a5

The Knight jumps aside and attacks the White Bishop.

13   d5-d6   Qc7-b8

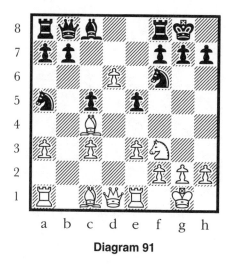

Diagram 91

A very sharp position. The chances are roughly equal. White's plan is to first safeguard his Bishop and then use his advantage in space to attack Black's unguarded central pawns at c5 and e5. Black will try to gang up on White's advanced pawn at d6 and pick it off. The ensuing play will blend strategy and tactics; both players will have to play accurately to maintain the balance.

GRUENFELD DEFENSE

The **Gruenfeld Defense** was invented in 1922 by the Austrian grandmaster Ernst Gruenfeld. It's characterized by these three moves:

1	d2-d4	Ng8-f6
2	c2-c4	g7-g6
3	Nb1-c3	d7-d5

Diagram 92

This defense incorporates a number of new ideas which we haven't seen before, so let's look closely at the rationale behind these moves.

In the openings we've looked at so far, Black has always made an effort to maintain a pawn in the center of the board. Sometimes, after various threats, Black has been forced to concede this pawn at a later stage of the opening, but usually at that point he's been able to carve out a share of the center.

In the **Gruenfeld Defense**, Black willingly concedes the entire center to White. The most common continuation from the last diagram, for instance, is...

4	c4xd5	Nf6xd5
5	e2-e4	Nd5xc3
6	b2xc3	

resulting in this position:

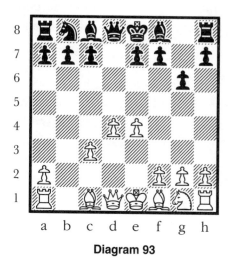

Diagram 93

Take a look. White's pawns apparently dominate the entire center, while Black has no visible presence at all. Can Black get away with such a strategy?

The answer, somewhat surprisingly, is a qualified "yes". Black hopes to demonstrate that White's pawn center is only apparently strong, and can actually become an object of attack. Black's plan is to continue with moves like Bf8-g7, 0-0, c7-c5, and Nb8-c6. Black's pieces and pawns will develop with an eye to undermining White's center from the flanks. If successful in this approach, Black hopes to gain strong central squares for his pieces after White's center has been compromised.

This general strategy is called **Hypermodernism**, and it came into vogue in the 1920s, and has remained with us ever since. Both the Gruenfeld Defense and the King's Indian Defense are founded on this principle. These openings are perfectly viable, but they require accurate and enterprising play. In return, they create double-edged positions and offer Black more winning chances than do other openings that we've considered.

The Gruenfeld Defense is an opening used by players who want a strong double-edged defense to d2-d4, with some immediate attacking chances for White but good play in the endgame for Black.

Let's continue from the last diagram and look at a typical development in the Gruenfeld Defense.

6	...	c7-c5

Black immediately starts the process of undermining White's center. If White captures with d4xc5, his pawn formation will be shattered and Black will soon regain the sacrificed pawn.

7	Bf1-c4

White develops his Bishop to its most aggressive square, bearing down on f7.

7	...	Bf8-g7

The Bishop adds its weight to the pressure against d4. This wing development of the Bishop is known as a **fianchetto.** Fianchettos are very popular in hypermodern openings.

8	Ng1-e2

This looks like a conservative development of the Knight, but there's a real point to it. White wants the Knight to support his pawn on d4, and he doesn't want Black to be able to pin the Knight by Bc8-g4, which would be possible if he developed the Knight to the usual square, f3. This way, Bc8-g4 on Black's part can be answered by f2-f3, chasing the Bishop away.

| 8 | ... | 0-0 |
| 9 | 0-0 | Nb8-c6 |

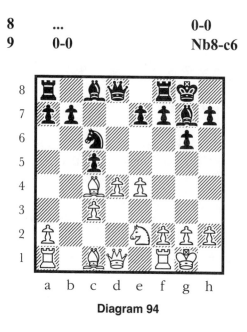

Diagram 94

Black continues to pile up on White's center. Now the d4-pawn is attacked four times, but defended only three times. White will have to move it or defend it.

10	Bc1-e3

White chooses to defend it again. White doesn't want to advance the pawn with d4-d5 because the great strength of a pawn center comes when the pawns are abreast at d4 and e4. Once White advances to d5, the squares at d6 and e5 become permanent posting spots for the Black pieces.

As before, White doesn't play d4xc5 because this would leave his pawn structure shattered and vulnerable to attack.

| 10 | ... | Qd8-c7 |

The Queen vacates the d8 square for the Black Rook.

| 11 | Ra1-c1 |

The White Rook takes up a position opposite the Black Queen. If the c-file ever opens, the Rook may generate some threats.

| 11 | ... | Nc6-a5 |

Black chases away the White Bishop.

| 12 | Bc4-d3 | b7-b6 |

Black prepares to fianchetto his other Bishop and strike at the White e-pawn.

| 13 | Qd1-d2 |

White gets the Queen off the first rank and connects the Rooks.

| 13 | ... | Bc8-b7 |

Black's Bishop takes up its position.

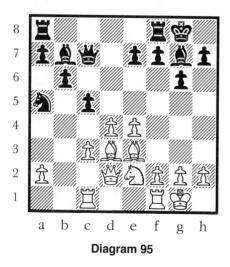

Diagram 95

The position is about even. Black's development and pressure balance out White's center control. White should proceed with a King's-side attack, with moves like f2-f4 and f4-f5. Black will counter in the center with Ra8-c8 and Rf8-d8, putting pressure on White's pawns.

KING'S INDIAN DEFENSE

The King's Indian Defense utilizes hypermodern principles in an even more radical fashion than the Gruenfeld. In the **King's Indian**, Black allows White to build a huge pawn center without opposition. The opening begins with these moves:

1	d2-d4	Ng8-f6
2	c2-c4	g7-g6
3	Nb1-c3	

So far, the same as in the Gruenfeld Defense. But now,

165

instead of lashing out in the center with d7-d5, Black simply continues his quiet development, allowing White to seize the entire center.

3	...	Bf8-g7
4	e2-e4	d7-d6
5	f2-f3	

This is the most aggressive way of proceeding against the King's Indian, although White can also try the quieter moves Ng1-f3 or Bf1-e2.

| 5 | ... | 0-0 |

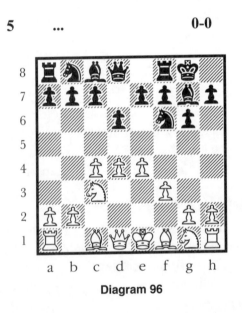

Diagram 96

Take a careful look at this last diagram. White has built a truly massive pawn center, while Black seems only to be fiddling on the edges of the board. But appearances in this case are deceiving: Black's position contains much latent dynamism, while White in many cases is hard-pressed to maintain his imposing formation.

Black has three possible plans for attacking the White center:

1. The advance c7-c5, followed by an attack on the Queen-side with a7-a6 and b7-b5.

2. The advance e7-e5, followed by a King-side attack with Nf6-h5 and f7-f5.

3. A liquidation of the center pawns, followed by an assault directly through the center to White's King.

The King's Indian Defense offers Black excellent winning chances but requires iron nerves. White's attacks are often ferocious, and Black must counterattack with equal verve or risk being blown off the board.

Let's take a look at a sample game, in which Black employs the third plan. In this game, the Black pieces were conducted by the late Mikhail Tal, an attacking genius who was World Champion from 1960 to 1961. The White pieces were handled by Szukszta of Poland. The game was played in 1956.

SZUKSZTA VS. TAL

	White (Szukszta)	Black (Tal)
1	d2-d4	Ng8-f6
2	c2-c4	g7-g6
3	Nb1-c3	Bf8-g7
4	e2-e4	d7-d6
5	f2-f3	0-0
6	Bc1-e3	e7-e5

167

Black finally starts action in the center. The plan that he will adopt depends on White's next move.

>   7   Ng1-e2

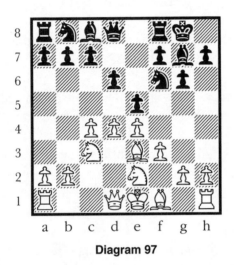

Diagram 97

White elects to maintain his pawns on d4 and e4 by supporting them with pieces. In this case, Black will try his third plan, opening the center. If White had played 7 d4-d5, Black would have opted for his second plan, attack on the King-side.

>   7   ...   c7-c6

This move prepares a later d6-d5 or perhaps b7-b5, depending on White's response.

>   8   Qd1-b3

An inaccurate move, since the Queen has nothing much to do over here. Better would have been 8 Qd1-d2.

8	...	e5xd4

Black starts his counter-attack by opening up the center.

9	Ne2xd4	d6-d5

This move involves a pawn sacrifice, since White attacks the d5 square four times, while Black defends it only three times. The plan, however, is to tear open the center files so Black's Rook (which will soon be on e8) can harass White's uncastled King.

10	c4xd5	c6xd5
11	e4xd5	

Diagram 98

11	...	Nb8-c6!

Amazing. Black sacrifices a Knight to continue the process of opening the center files.

12 d5xc6

Why not? When in doubt - accept your opponent's sacrifices. Make him prove he knows what he's doing.

12 ... Rf8-e8

The point of Black's previous move. He threatens both Re8xe3 check and Qd8xd4, since the Bishop is now pinned to the King.

13 Ke1-f2

White breaks the pin and defends the Bishop, but at the cost of forfeiting the right to castle.

13 ... Re8xe3!

Black smashes through the White position with this sacrifice of Rook for Bishop.

14 Ra1-d1

White doesn't want to get drawn into the complications of 14 Kf2xe3 Bg7-h6 check 15 f3-f4 Nf6-g5 check, when all of Black's pieces are buzzing around the White King. His actual move looks like a winner, since White now threatens both Kf2xe3 and c6xb7.

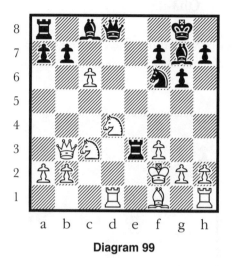

Diagram 99

| 14 | ... | Nf6-g4 check! |

The attack continues in brilliant fashion. Black sacrifices a Knight to uncover the Bishop on g7.

| 15 | f3xg4 | Bg7xd4 |

Black has many threats, the most serious being Re3xc3 discovered check.

| 16 | Rd1xd4 |

White gives back a Rook for a Bishop in order to stem the tide.

| 16 | ... | Qd8xd4 |

Still threatening Re3xc3 check.

171

17   Qb3-d5

This threat of exchanging Queens looks like it may beat off the attack, but Black has another stunning surprise ready.

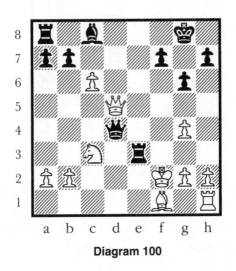

Diagram 100

17   ...   Re3-e2
                                         double check!!

Amazing. Black sacrifices his Rook to get the White King to a square where the Bishop can attack it with check.

18   Kf2xe2

White can only escape a double check by moving his King.

18   ...   **Bc8xg4 check**

172

19	Ke2-e1	Ra8-e8 check

20	Bf1-e2	

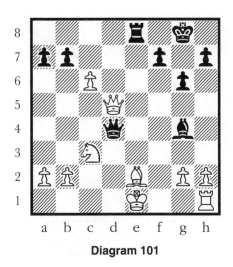

Diagram 101

Has White escaped?

20	...	Re8xe2 check!

The final brilliant point. If White tries Nc3xe2, Black has Qd4xd5, with a winning advantage of a Queen for a Rook. Instead, White resigns.

A marvelous game, typical of Tal at his most incandescent.

9

NEXT STEPS

That wraps up our survey of chess openings. If you've worked your way this far, you now have a good grasp of the ideas behind more than two dozen different openings.

cardozabooks.com
Go to www.cardozabooks.com to get more information about Bill Robertie's great chess books and to order them direct from the publisher.

At this point, you should be able to select some openings which fit your style, and which will cause lots of problems for your less sophisticated opponents.

You may also want to take a look at our book, *Beginning Chess Play*. Pay particular attention to the discussion on chess tactics in the General Winning Strategy chapter, and carefully work through the two complete annotated games. You'll find the material an excellent complement to what you've learned so far in this book.

Now you'll have to get out and actually play some chess. Look for a chess club in your area (*Beginning Chess Play* has some useful tips for tracking them down). Challenge people to play. With the knowledge you've acquired here, winning will be easier than you think. If there are some really good players in your area, sit down and watch them play. Try to learn some of their tricks and techniques, and see if you can incorporate them in your own games.

Keep playing, keep learning, and keep winning!